MINIATURE
ROOM
SETTINGS

MINIATURE ROOM SETTINGS

Helen Ruthberg

Chilton Book Company *Radnor, Pennsylvania*

Photographs by Helen Karp Ruthberg
unless otherwise indicated

Library of Congress Catalog Card Number 77-14742
ISBN 0-8019-6678-7 *Casebound Edition*
ISBN 0-8019-6679-5 *Paperback*

Manufactured in the United States of America

2 3 4 5 6 7 8 9 0   7 6 5 4 3 2 1 0 9

With affection . . .
For the two most important men in my life:
my husband, JACK, and son, BRADFORD.

Note to Readers

There's no doubt about it!

Miniatures have captured the hearts of all the people. Generations have discovered that miniaturing is undoubtedly the most intriguing activity to come along in decades. Whether it's active participation or passive admiration, the miniature has produced an avalanche of joy for grandchild and grandparent, male and female, healthy and afflicted. Whether collecting miniatures or creating one's own, this charming and beautiful hobby has reached out to the masses, enabling many to achieve big goals in a very small way.

The field of miniatures is limited only by one's imagination. For many, this book will serve as an introduction. For others, it will open a whole new dimension in miniatures. Because of the wealth of ideas and information to be shared with you, the readers, I have limited the repetition of instructions from my first book, *The Book of Miniatures: Furniture and Accessories*. While each book stands on its own, I encourage you to refer to the more than 1000 ideas, hints and suggestions put forth in my first book.

Acknowledgments

Assistance comes in many different roles and I am grateful to many people for their selfless offerings. Special thanks are extended to the following:

Sybil Harp, Editor of *Creative Crafts* and *The Miniature Magazine*, and Carstens Publishing Company for permission to include portions of articles and photographs which originally appeared in their publications.

The Phoenix Art Museum, Phoenix, Arizona, for permission to use photographs of rooms by Mrs. James Ward Thorne.

Peter F. Westcott was a sympathetic and excellent liaison.

Norman Forgue promptly and generously provided aid as needed. He also granted permission for use of quotations from the book *Gems of Thought*, compiled and edited by Walter Norman May, published by Normandie House, Chicago.

Lydia Driscoll, Senior Editor of Chilton Book Company, the perfect author's editor, was always ready to cooperate and be understanding.

Rhoda and Norman Pollock processed my films and found me an "improved student."

Donna Murray of Fabric-Craft Outlet continued to spoil me with her generosity.

Ernie Levy shared some of his remarkable expertise.

Angelina Rudden provided her lovely hands for photographic needs, enhancing each picture.

Miniaturists shared their creations and are credited where their work is shown.

Family, friends and acquaintances offered encouragement and moral support . . . especially Ilse Goldsmith, Roberta Moore and Edith Gillman.

My husband, Jack, maintained a calm and patient attitude and now looks forward to a return to normalcy—if that is possible.

Contents

List of Illustrations

List of Color Illustrations

PART I

Creating Rooms in Miniature

*Find out what you want to do, and then do it!
. . . It is boredom that wears a man down, not
the fatigue of sustained effort he enjoys.*
F. ALEXANDER MAGOUN (1896–   )

CHAPTER
1

The Single Room

APPEAL AND ADVANTAGES

Dollhouses do have their own special appeal. They bring order into the life of a miniature world. There are rooms for preparing food, for eating, for sleeping, for cleansing, for socializing; all the daily commitments of various lifestyles are brought together under one tiny structure.

But, there are other modes of miniaturing that exert their own special appeal and these are the single room units which can't begin to be classified in any one way, since they represent a variety of conditions related to living, working, playing, entertaining and, yes, even existing.

The single room may exemplify one room of a home and, depending upon the whim of the creator, this may take shape in a period or modern setting. Or the "room," loosely termed, may represent a shop or office or amusement area—but no matter "what," the individual unit becomes something very special and very much enjoyed.

There are definite advantages to miniaturing with one room. *Size, variety,* *placement* and *portability* are the major attributes.

Size

What is an appropriate size for a box? It varies according to what you want. The depth of a box is the feature that distinguishes a room from a vignette. A vignette is narrow, approximately ranging from 2″ to 4″ (Fig. 1–1). The depth of a room can vary with the requirements of the room design, but 12″ is practical and logical for most rooms. A 12″-deep box will often fit easily on the shelf of a large bookcase or, if several rooms are planned, the conformity and appearance of one depth is very pleasing to the eye.

Normally, a room may be from 8″ to 12″ in height, with some very elegant rooms being even higher. But, and I say this unequivocally, I make *all* my rooms at least 12″ high because it's much easier to see into the room once it is finished.

The width of a box is variable and, although 20″ is much to my liking, again this depends upon what you per-

Fig. 1–1 An 8″ x 10″ reverse-scoop frame is large enough to hold a few miniature items and look interesting against a fabric background. This 2″-deep vignette contains a wall full of pieces handmade by the author. The Columbian chair and seashell basket (an earring) are purchases.

sonally choose to put into the area. Commonsense tells you that some rooms are uncluttered, while others demand more space.

Variety

Do miniature rooms have to be repetitious? Absolutely not! Variety is one of the greatest assets of the single room. Although we may all experience the same emotions of happiness, sadness, grief and love, our experiences and responses for one thing or another are vastly different. Hence our taste in rooms will vary. How you touch down and associate in life may well determine what you decide to create in a room. Personal living conditions, real or unreal, can manifest themselves and the miniaturist may soon find that her own life is entwined within a miniature domain.

Since I am an artist, it was inevitable that an artist's studio was created. For an avid seashell collector, the seashell shop was also an automatic response to a loving hobby. I won't try to account for my other miniature endeavors at this time, but whether a room reflects the past, present or future, each little masterpiece becomes something special for you and for others to see.

Placement

Where can a box be displayed? An acquaintance recently told me that if

Fig. 1-2 At left is an entrance hall to a Victorian living room with "acquired heirlooms." Notice the "Roots" photograph of great-grandparents and their grown children on the back wall.

she made a box room she'd put it right on the dining room table for everyone to see. Of course that's one solution, but your box can be placed anywhere that will accommodate its size. Almost any free-standing piece of furniture, such as a table, buffet, etagere, credenza, bureau, bookcase (with good depth), fern stand or floor-based stereo speaker, will prove useful (Fig. 1–3). The door to a closet can be cut into. With proper carpentry work, a rectangular slot can be cut out of the door. A shadowbox can be constructed and supported from the inside. One, two or three rooms can be displayed this way. Wall shelves can be planned and properly spaced for displaying rooms; but be careful of triangular support brackets that tend to cut into the placement

Fig. 1–3 A stereo speaker provides a perfect base for displaying a single room unit. The predominantly white interior is extended to outside of box, covered with white ceiling wallpaper. Two white-and-gold baroque handles are added to sides for easy carrying.

area. Have you a spare closet or can you sacrifice one for your minis? Have shelves set in, extending from side to side. An old bureau with annoying, sticky drawers can have the insides pulled out and be redone with shelving. A strong bracket shelf may be specially built.

Without straining the back and twisting the neck, eye-level viewing is the ideal way to gape at miniatures. One answer lies in having specially constructed cubicles along a wall. An entrance hall or extra-wide hallway might be available for such carpentry work or there may be other areas that lend themselves to suitable display pieces.

When I had an exhibition, a young state trooper, on his one day off, graciously built a special display piece to accommodate four rooms (Fig. 1–4). Wayne Akstin was ingenious in his selection of materials. Keeping cost down, he selected 2″-wide Styrofoam used as insulation in homebuilding. He cleverly mounted a pine board within the Styrofoam structure and cut out four apertures, to accommodate four framed box rooms, easily inserted and easily removed when necessary.

Some miniature rooms are planned to go inside a cupboard or the empty shell of a clock, radio or television set. For clear vision without using walls, a fish tank might even prove adaptable for some special theme, such as a picnic or a beautiful garden. The glass domes usually placed over lovely clock cases can likewise be placed over a miniature arrangement. We could also benefit from the way a sculptor exhibits—construct a simple sculptor's stand.

What is the greatest advantage of a box room? No doubt, it's *portability*. You certainly won't need any help moving a single room from place to

Fig. 1–4 A unique arrangement for exhibiting miniature rooms was originated by Wayne Akstin. He selected 2″-thick Styrofoam sheets, used in homebuilding insulation, for the rectangular top piece. Bases and two upright sculpture stands of wood complete the display.

place. Lightweight, compact and, provided all the inside elements are fastened securely in place, your one-room creation can be tenderly handled with two steady, loving hands.

Easy to take to house parties, shows, conferences, displays, meetings, nursing homes and even family get-togethers, your little room can travel and *enjoy* being admired, too. That may sound silly, but I don't think of rooms as inanimate objects—not with all the "living and activity" that seems to be going on within a well-planned tiny area. All things considered, an un-

encumbered box remains the best solution for the person who would like to transport her displays easily.

INSPIRATION

Variety is described in the dictionary as "the absence of sameness." Sameness is dull and there's no reason for miniature rooms to be multiplied over and over with the same room settings, same color schemes and same furniture. Stop and think! How many real homes or offices are *exactly* duplicated in our world? Aside from commercially preplanned, furnished-for-rent apartments,

I don't see how any two persons could ever *exactly* have the same room. So why do this in miniature? Be assertive, be an individual, be imaginative and "do your own thing."

Inspiration pops up unexpectedly. I knew I wanted to do a room with food, but how? One day when my husband and I were eating in a restaurant, the appealing, rather formal interior design provided the catalyst and it was then that the idea of a smorgasbord was born.

There's no explaining how, when or why you will arrive at an idea, but to help get your thought vibrations activated, I've compiled a list of possibilities. Perhaps one of these will spark some initiative and encourage you to begin.

Rooms of a Home from Any Era

    Attic
    Basement
    Bathroom or powder room
    Billiard room
    Bedroom
    Chauffeur's room
    Den
    Dining room or breakfast nook
    Family room
    Foyer or entrance hall
    Game room
    Garage
    Garden room
    Kitchen
    Pantry or butler's pantry
    Laundry room
    Library
    Living room, sitting room, parlor, drawing room or salon
    Maid's room
    Music room
    Nursery
    Patio
    Porch
    Sauna
    Sewing room

    Sun parlor or solarium
    Trophy room
    Wine cellar
    Workshop

Period Rooms

    Apothecary shop
    Ballroom
    Blacksmith shop
    Cabinetmaker's shop
    Candle shop
    Chandler's shop
    Comb shop
    Cooper's shop
    Corset shop
    General store
    Gun shop
    Leather shop
    Locksmith
    Millinery shop
    Pewter shop
    Physician's office
    Print shop
    Seamstress shop
    Silversmith shop
    Stable
    Tailor shop
    Tavern or saloon
    Turner's shop
    Weaver's shop
    Wheelwright shop
    Wigmaker's shop
    Woodcarver's shop

Businesses, Stores and Showrooms

    Antique repair shop
    Antique shop
    Appliance showroom
    Auto body repair shop
    Auto dealer
    Auto parts store
    Bakery
    Bank
    Barber shop
    Bath shop
    Beauty salon (hair stylist)
    Bedding shop
    Bicycle shop
    Boat showroom

Fig. 1–5 The Antique Shop is often a favorite among miniaturists, probably because all those collectible miniature items eventually find a home. Norman Forgue, creator of this charming example, provides an interesting array of 127 items. Display cases, tables and many of the pieces shown are made of anything from hairpins to buttons. An interesting front display area is kept open, allowing full view of lighted shop interior. (*Larry DeVera, photograph*)

Book store or used-book store
Boutique
Bowling equipment store
Bridal shop
Brokerage firm
Brush shop
Butcher shop
Candy shop
Carpenter's shop
Cheese shop
China shop
Christmas shop
Clock shop
Clothing shop—for children and infants, women, men
Cosmetic shop
Costume rental agency
Craft shop
Curtain and drapery store
Dive shop
Doll shop
Dollhouse and miniature shop
Drugstore
Dry cleaner
Egg wholesaler
Fabric store
Fence dealer
Fireplace and hearth equipment store
Fish and seafood store
Flower and plant shop
Formal-wear rental agency
Frame shop
Fruit and vegetable market
Furniture store
Furniture stripping and refinishing shop or unfinished furniture store
Garden center
Gasoline station
Gift shop
Glass and mirror store
Grocery store (Ma and Pa store)
Gun shop
Hardware store
Hat shop
Health food store
Hobby and model shop
Import shop
Interior decorating shop
Ironworks
Jewelry shop

Junk store
Kennel and cattery
Lamp and lighting store
Laundromat
Laundry
Leather store
Linen shop
Lingerie and corset shop
Liquor store
Locksmith shop
Luggage store
Lumberyard
Mason equipment company
Maternity shop
Millwork company
Mineral and gem shop
Monument company
Motorcycle store
Musical instrument store
Needlework shop
Office supplies store
Organ store
Oriental shop
Paint and wallpaper store
Pastry shop
Pawn shop
Perfume shop
Repair shop
Rug, carpet and linoleum shop
Saddlery and harness shop
Seashell shop
Service station
Sewing machine shop
Shoemaker
Shoestore
Sporting goods store
Stamp and coin store
Stationery and card store
Stereo equipment store
Supermarket
Tailor shop
Telephone company
Television store
Tire store
Tobacco shop
Toy store
Travel agency
Trim and button shop
Trophy shop
Tropical fish store

Uniform shop
Upholstery shop
Variety shop
Wig shop

Educational Settings

Beauty school
Conference room
Conservatory
Convention room
Display room
Gymnasium
Kindergarten
Laboratories
Nursery school

School classroom (academic, college and university, medical school, dental school)
Seminar room
Technical and trade school (beauty, culinary, dance, karate, secretarial)

Fantasy Rooms

Candy factory
Castle or palace
Elfland
Futurity Room 3000
Heaven
Mouse house room
Outer Space Room 2000

Fig. 1–6 Norman Forgue labels his Service Shop "one of the *fun* things"; it is 3¹/₂″ deep. (*Larry DeVera, photograph*)

Purgatory
Santa Claus' Workshop
Science Fiction Creations

Foreign Rooms

English pub
French cafe
French cancan show
Geisha room
German beer garden
Greek temple
Japanese garden
Japanese sitting room
Mexican shop

Historical Rooms

Edison home and laboratory
Fort
Frontier housing
Indian settlement
Military headquarters
Monticello
Mount Vernon
Betsy Ross room
West Point
White House room
Williamsburg

Miscellaneous

Art show (clothes line exhibit, school
    children's art)
Auction gallery
Ballroom
Barn
Campground
College student's room or dormitory
Clubroom
Famous person's room
Farmer's market
Farmyard
Fencing salon
Flea market
Fruit storage
Garage sale
Gazebo
Greenhouse
Health spa
Hotel/motel room
Lighthouse

Marina
Merry-go-round
Mill (grist mill)
Miniaturist at work
Mobile home
Nursing home
Outhouse
Party
Picnic
Prom
Scrap metal yard
Showroom
Ski lodge
Tackroom
Treehouse
Winery

Professional Offices

Accountant's office
Advertising studio
Artist's studio (commercial)
Banker's office
Dentist's office
Doctor's office
Editor's office
Engineer's office
Insurance company
Lawyer's office
Optometrist's office
Photographer's studio
Principal's office
Publisher's office
Real estate office
Sculptor's studio
Veterinarian's office

Public Places

Airport (hangar, tower)
Band park circle or gazebo
Bus depot
Cemetery or mausoleum
Courtroom
Employment agency
Firehouse
Funeral home
Gallery (art, sculpture)
Hospital (waiting room, patient's
    room, surgical, X-ray, laboratory)
Hotel lobby

Fig. 1–7 Among the vignette rooms that Norman Forgue has created is a series of Raggedy Ann and Andy. This one shows the famous girl and boy dolls in their playroom. (*Larry DeVera, photograph*)

Jail
Library
Mortuary
Museum (art, sculpture, artifacts, period, wax)
Newsstand
Police station
Post office
Railroad station
Town hall

Religious Scenes

Baptism
Bar Mitzvah
Buddhist ceremony
Chapel
Choir

Crèche
Holidays (Christmas, Easter, Passover, Succoth)
House of worship
Monastery
Pulpit of church or synagogue
Vestry
Wedding

Restaurants

Bar and grill
Cafeteria
Chinese or Polynesian restaurant
Delicatessen
Diner
Doughnut shop
Drive-in

German rathskeller
Gypsy tearoom
Ice cream parlor or soda fountain
Luncheonette
Outdoor cafe
Pizzeria
Saloon
Sandwich shop
Seafood restaurant
Smorgasbord
Stands (hot dog, ice cream, ices, cotton candy, pizza)

Scandalous Rooms
Bordello
Gambling casino
Massage parlor
Mistress' bedroom
Speakeasy

Storybook Settings
Adventure stories (James Bond 007)
Arabian nights
Cartoons (Flintstones, Flash Gordon, Alley Oop)
Children's stories (*Peter Pan, Tom Sawyer, Alice in Wonderland*)
Classics (Shakespeare, etc.)
Detective stories (Sherlock Holmes, Sam Spade, Fu Manchu)

Fairy tales
Fantasies (*The Hobbit*)
Fiction (*Gone with the Wind, Wuthering Heights*)
Nursery rhymes

Theater, Entertainment and Sports Scenes
Arcade (juke box, pinball machine)
Billiard parlor
Bowling alley
Burlesque
Carnival
Circus
Dance ballroom
Dance studio
Follies
Medicine man show
Minstrel show
Movie set
Movie theater
Musical or dramatic set
Night club
Opera
Puppet show (marionettes)
Radio station
Rinks (ice skating, roller skating)
Rodeo
Star's dressing room
Summer Theater (tent)
Television set or show

CHAPTER
2

Tools and Supplies

Fine feathers make fine birds and good tools help make good work. The selection of your wood, the sharpness of your implements, the strength of your glue, the quality of your paper and fabrics, all combine to help produce an acceptable piece of miniature work.

Most miniaturists already have a workshop well in order, whether it's in a basement, attic room, extra room, garage, closet, kitchen area or a small cubbyhole sequestered away in the corner of a family room. And, while most established miniaturists already have their tools well accounted for, I'll list the essentials for the benefit of newcomers.

Tools and supplies are broken down into different categories to help determine what you may already have available and what may have to be purchased. Your own interest and direction is the best decision-maker regarding choice of tools and supplies, as you will ultimately discover.

STANDARD MATERIALS LISTS

Household Supplies

Round toothpicks (for applying glue and making small structures)

Poultry skewer or large drapery hook (substitutes for awl; when heated, will pierce plastic)

Long, pointed tweezers for placing small items in position

Waxed paper to glue on; wax resists sticking

Scissors, regular and cuticle; latter will cut thin metal

Used ballpoint pen for many purposes

Pencils (hard and medium hard)

Eraser

Tape measure

Masking tape

Cellophane tape

Mystik tape

Cotton balls and cotton batting; help when gluing items together

Foam rubber

Permanent-color felt nibbed markers (Sharpie)

Emery boards

Cutting board of smooth vinyl tile

Clip clothespins and hair clips for clamping

Paper clips

Straight pins

Rubber bands

Small juice cans

Empty deodorant jars with lids (to keep mixed paint from drying out)

Paper toweling and rags

Fig. 2–1 Straight pins, hairspray and a corrugated box are humble household supplies that help in miniaturing. Shown are a pair of curtains hung on a dowel stick, stretched and held in place with pins. Sprayed a few times, the material is stiff enough to remain in place.

Applicator sticks, tongue depressors, Popsicle sticks
Lestoil (cleans brushes)
Nail polish remover (cleans fingers)
Hairspray (stiffens fabric folds of curtains or hanging garments)

Stationery, Art and Craft Items

Illustration board
3-ply Bristol board (used for backing purposes)
File cards (referred to as card in text)
9″ x 12″ sketch pad
9″ x 12″ tracing paper pad
Graph paper
Drawing compass

Drawing pencils (HB, H and 2H)
Paper punch
Ticket punch (round hole)
T square
Dividers
Stylus (small nib)
Brushes: rounds #000, #0, #3, others; brights #00, #2, others; Aquarelle, 1″ size

Glues

Titebond, Elmer's Glue-All, Weldbond, Sobo for wood bonding purposes
Franklin Liquid Hide Glue for bonding edges of box rooms

Duco Cement and Scotch Super-Strength Adhesive for general bonding purposes

Epoxy glue for bonding large, heavy structures together, bonding porous to nonporous material

Instant bond adhesives for a small, *quick* setup

Velverette for bonding fabric

Testors polystyrene glue for plastics

Cutting and Workshop Tools

X-acto knife and blades (carving tools)

X-acto miter box

X-acto soldering iron and hot knife

Jeweler's saw

Single-edged razor blades (several)

Pliers—chain nose and serrated jaw types

Diagonal semiflush wire cutter

Gripping pliers

Electrician's pliers with side cutter

Wire cutter

Needle files

Hammer

Hand drill

Vacuum vise

Brads and nails

Electric and Battery-Operated Power Tools

Jigsaw (Dremel Moto-Shop)

Drill (Dremel Moto-Tool)

Lathe (Dremel Moto-Lathe)

Finishing Products

Sandpapers: good quality *medium* (for box); *fine* and *very fine* for furniture

Steel wool, #0000

Paints: acrylic paint in tubes and jars (art and crafts stores); gesso (undercoat), Liquitex for acrylic; Testors PLA enamels (also gold and silver); black India ink; X-acto stains

Stains: walnut, mahogany, others (Minwax)

Shellac

Polyurethane varnish (satin finish, gloss finish)

Clear acrylic spray

Finishing wax (Minwax)

Soft polishing cloth

Woods

Wood is usually obtained after the decision is made to construct a specific project.

Balsa—softwood, easily cut with a craft knife or single-edge razor blade; available in several sizes; sold in sheets and strips at hobby and craft stores; useful for furniture, accessory and interior construction

Spruce—medium-hard wood; sold in sheets and strips in better hobby and model shops

Basswood—medium-hard wood; sold in sheets and strips; available from dealers; this wood is usually used in commercial kits

Cherry, Walnut, Mahogany, Oak, Hard Pine, etc.—hardwoods of fine and coarse grain; require a power tool for cutting; available in blocks or sheets of limited sizes from advertised dealers or from local cabinetmakers

Dowels—hardwood with diameters of $3/32''$, $1/8''$, $3/16''$, $1/4''$, $3/8''$, $1/2''$, $3/4''$; very useful in miniature work; available in hardware and lumber stores

Plywood—available in thicknesses of $1/8''$, $1/4''$, etc., and in various woods; useful for wall construction purposes within room when covered over with paper or paint

HELPFUL HINTS

• Tools tend to be buried under accumulating debris that piles up in miniature work and time is spent looking for them. A large-size organizer drawer tray is helpful for keeping your working surface orderly. Fill the sections with various working tools, including the humble toothpick. When finished using scissors, clippers, glue, cotton or card,

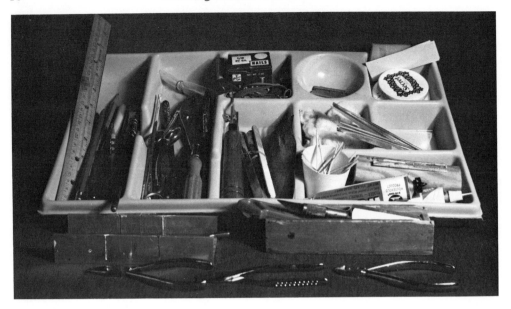

Fig. 2–2 A drawer organizer tray holds essential small working tools and supplies. Replacing items in tray helps to develop better working habits.

Fig. 2–3 An easily assembled door kit from Scale Model Supplies is laid out in a box or box cover on top of graph paper and waxed paper. Lines of graph paper assure proper alignment. This is helpful for making furniture and frames, too.

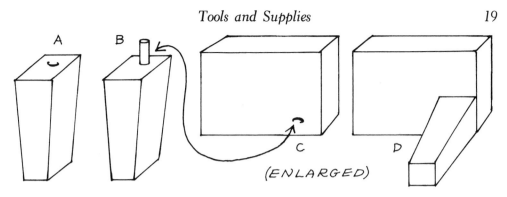

Fig. 2–4 Steps in pegging furniture to attach posts, legs and arms.

return to a sectioned area. This certainly improves working habits. Thinking it over, *two* trays might even be better.

• Trays are also good for holding pieces of wood for special cutout projects which should be separated from other cutout designs.

• To keep squeezing out small mounds of glue is sometimes annoying. Pour a small amount into a plastic pill container with an old-fashioned, easy snap-off lid. It is just the right size for dipping a toothpick into, which eliminates the squeeze-wait period. The glue remains fresh when the lid is replaced.

• Gluing horizontal and vertical pieces together can sometimes result in lopsided projects. To keep parts straight, tape graph paper down first and tape waxed paper on top to the inside surface of a box. (Fig. 2–3). The working project fits snugly on the bottom *against* the "wall" of the box; the graph paper helps vertical-horizontal structures remain straight. The waxed paper resists glue-sticking problems.

• *Pegging* your furniture will prevent posts, legs or arms from eventually breaking loose and makes for a better quality piece of work. A simple method is to drill a small hole in one side of object (A), insert and glue a cut round toothpick (B). Clip off rest of toothpick,

leaving about $1/8''$ protruding. Drill hole in area where object is to be adhered (C) and insert and glue toothpick end (D).

• Covering interior walls with paper or cloth can either be fun or frustrating. Conducting an experiment, I found that one little detail made a vast difference in application of wall covering, producing a smooth surface. If the dry paper was applied directly onto the glued area, I invariably ended up with ripples on the surface, but, if I quickly immersed the paper in water, shook out the excess moisture and laid the paper into proper position, which is easier to do when it's wet, then I was more successful. The paper is pressed smooth with a brayer. Fingers and paper toweling also help push out bubbles and excess moisture in corners. This has worked well with commercial wallpaper, which is sturdy, but greater care must be exercised with the special miniature papers; since they are more fragile, extra wetness could cause tears. Works very well with fabrics, too.

• Use diluted white glue, with or without colored acrylic paint, to help stiffen working materials that are too flexible. Materials are held in position; ribbons and lace trims can be shaped into curves, squares or whatever is needed.

CHAPTER
3

Architectural Detailing

The architect utilizes experience and knowledge to provide homes of charm and grace. Applying architectural design within a room "opens many doors" and the *final* concept of a room is determined by era, culture, heritage and financial resources.

Miniature rooms borrow from their full-size counterparts and, unless you're copying a room from your own real home, you'll probably want to research your needs. This is most applicable to period and special rooms of historical nature. Just as fashion changes in clothing, so does fashion change in architecture and, while some styles have altered in appearance or been laid to rest, others continue to endure in the building industry.

PERIOD STYLES

Early American and Colonial

Very *Early American* architecture, if one can call it that, was a primitive shelter and dealt with the necessities of life. Timber interiors, enormous stone fireplaces, large-plank wooden floors and hand-hewn beamed ceilings were some of the basics for a hardy existence.

A hefty wooden door and an inadequate number of small windows with small panes of glass provided protection from inclement weather and enemies.

Colonial is an ongoing style with emphasis on simplicity and serenity. The early rectangular frame also produced the saltbox profile and the Cape Cod style, each providing four functional rooms situated around a fireplace in the central stack. Four rooms on both first and second floors provided ample living space. The stairway was situated opposite the front door and next to the stack. Stairways were constructed of wood and were either closed or open-string stairs. Balusters ranged from simple rectangular posts to intricately turned designs. Windows were small panes of glass and construction was simple.

Georgian

The *Georgian* period, a part of the Colonial era, gained popularity during the reigns of George I, II and III from 1714 to 1795. A taste for finer living prevailed and carvings and stucco ornamentation became lavish on ceilings.

20

Fig. 3–1 Early American architecture depended largely upon settlers from England and the Continent. *English Jacobean Hall (1603–1649)* is one of the rooms by Mrs. James Ward Thorne which is displayed at the Phoenix Art Museum. This is a copy of a room in Levens Hall, Westmoreland, in which the paneling, wainscoting and furniture were all made of oak. Richly carved wood and paneling is evident in the mantel and over-mantel; other features of the Jacobean period are seen in Italian Renaissance and Gothic design. (*Augustus Beinlich, photograph; courtesy of Phoenix Art Museum*)

Early Georgian houses defined fireplaces, windows and doorways with classical moldings. Pilasters of either rectangular or half-round columns were very much a part of wall construction, as were pediments, triangular tops above doors. Early homes boasted fully paneled rooms, later domiciles only paneled fireplace walls. Plaster walls followed, accompanied by cornices, dados and chair rails; the painted plaster was later papered with large scenic designs. The lower portion of wall, called wainscoting, was either flat paneled or paneled with wood, creating a raised effect through tapering or with the use of molding.

Mantelpieces were ornately designed of Italian marble, chimney pieces featured carved designs and decorative inlays enhanced formal wooden floors. Fireplaces were smaller in living quarters and a wide central hall was popular, connecting front to back.

Sash windows made an appearance, but multiple panes of glass were used. Twelve panes each were required until 1840, then the number was reduced to six panes for each window. Beautiful Palladian windows graced handsome staircases, second floor hallways or a very special room. Fan-light windows topped doorways and tall, narrow sidelight windows were used to the left and right of doors.

Decorative inlays enhanced formal wooden floors. Cheaper imitations were effected by painting simulated designs of tiles, marble and parquet directly on the floor. Rug designs were painted on canvas floor coverings, but this is related to interior design—not necessarily to architectural detail.

Furniture related to the Georgian period is Queen Anne, Chippendale, Hepplewhite and Sheraton.

American Federal

With American independence, a new nation came into being and along with it came a new style in architecture—or perhaps I should say revival neo-Greek and neo-Roman. The *American Federal* period (French Empire and English Regency) flourished from about 1785 to 1840. Most influential was Robert Adam, whose designs became fashionable in both architecture and furniture.

This was a period of delicacy and refinement, replacing rococo design. Ionic columns dominated the classic motif, with pilasters, arches and niches being used generously. Roman classic motives, such as scrolls, swags, festoons, wreaths and laurel, branches, torches and mythological figures, were very much a part of architectural interiors, but decorative details and moldings were minimized. Unobtrusive fireplace mantels were made of marble and simple moldings.

Pilasters, often fluted, continued to be used, not only on walls but as panels flanking a door or window or as part of a fireplace mantel. Some rooms took on a new shape, becoming oval or quadrangular. Windows were large and expansive and the bay window appeared on the scene. Walls were mostly plaster, painted or papered, with an occasional use of elaborate paneling decorated with motif.

The eagle, America's national bird, became a symbolic part of the Federal period. As heavier Empire progressed, decline had set in by 1830, but Thomas Jefferson's Monticello remains a living monument to this prestigious era.

Furniture related to the Federal period is Adam, Hepplewhite, Sheraton (Directoire) and Duncan Phyfe (Regency).

Fig. 3–2 *English Georgian Library* (1714–1820) from the Thorne Rooms Collection is a fine example of a well-balanced, serene and orderly room. Beautiful carving is evident in the mantel and above the door. The bookcase niche and adjoining tall windows feature curved semicircular arches.

Against a background of painted plastic walls, furnishings are examples of Queen Anne and Thomas Chippendale design. (*Augustus Beinlich, photograph; courtesy of Phoenix Art Museum*)

Victorian

Enter *Victorian* from 1840 to 1901. Great changes were wrought by the Industrial Revolution. Mass-produced moldings, pressings and castings were cheap. Hence interiors were heavily laden with wooden ornamentation. Walls and ceilings were profusely decorated and imitations of expensive wood and marble were painted on plaster and wallboards.

Victorian, with baroque and rococo styles, reflected French, Italian and Roman influences. Neo-Gothic played a role in design, with use of Tudor arch panels for doorways, windows and chimney pieces. Ceilings in very elegant homes were high, ribbed and vaulted. Mantels were usually of marble, elaborately designed and carved.

The fitted bathroom was first introduced in elegant homes, becoming commonplace as the Victorian era ended. Central-heating systems were installed; built-in closets, cupboards and pantries solved increasing storage problems; *and*, by 1900, electricity was proven effective. Oh, happy day!

By Victorian times, window glass was produced in larger sizes and a sash window was usually made of two vertical panes joined by mutin. By 1880, a single pane of glass was available. The unique contribution to windows was the use of stained glass. Translucent mosaic patterns or pictorial renditions were beautifully designed, much credited to the talent of Louis Comfort Tiffany.

Oak became so popular that eventually the era was referred to as the Golden Oak period. Doors and window sashes made much use of this wood, as did the furniture designers of the day. Furniture related to this period is Belter, Thonet, Eastlake and Morris.

Art Nouveau and Contemporary

Toward the end of the Victorian era, new expressions were again being voiced architecturally. Two attitudes prevailed. One segment of realists wanted a national style related to classic elements of the past. But the arts and crafts movement in England of the latter nineteenth century was bound to have an effect. Consequently, *art nouveau,* a separatist movement, came into being. Rejecting the excessive ornamentation of Victorian, "new-thinking" designs were introduced, returning to the simple natural lines of flowers and fruit and the peacock. Lines were long, flowing and curvilinear, ending abruptly in a whiplike curve. Huge decorative panels or massive mirrors adorned the walls. Delicate moldings overlaid mirrors and wound around corners and pillars. Iron decorations were much in evidence, especially in the structure of stairways, elevators and balconies. Double-hung windows were often enhanced by stained-glass decorations and etched glass became an added feature.

By 1902, a simpler rectilinear manner was more in vogue and, by 1913, the art nouveau movement had wilted.

Furniture related to this period is Van de Velde, Thonet and Tiffany.

There is usually an overlapping of architectural periods. Just when the *international style* began is arguable, but it did have its inception during the Edwardian era.

Functionalism became important and the notable change in architecture is that ornamentation vanished. About 1930, a new style called *streamlining* evolved, producing a sleek, tapered look with an unquestionably modern appearance.

Fig. 3–3 Classic revival of Greek and Roman architecture is evident in the charm and beauty of an *English-Adam Dining Room*. This Thorne Room exemplifies the remarkable talent of Robert Adam (1728–1792) as architect, interior designer and furniture designer. Classic influence is displayed through use of painted furniture, inlaid satin wood and ornamental plastic medallions. The white medallions and pilasters accent the gray walls. The white and black marble floor is accented with a needlepoint rug. (*Augustus Beinlich, photograph; courtesy of Phoenix Art Museum*)

Unadorned materials were now accepted for interior use and multitudinous new supplies were used in aesthetic ways. Brick, stone, marble, slate, wood, ceramic, masonry and other materials were appreciated for their intrinsic beauty.

Houses were planned for the individual needs of the family, becoming simpler, direct and natural. Functional designs provided built-ins, producing workable areas such as kitchens. Rooms opened up to the outside, separated by large areas of glass, placing the family in contact with nature. The patio replaced the porch and that is a loss.

Inside, walls were variable, including veneers, plywood, gypsum board, sheetrock—painted, papered or covered with burlap. Some special rooms even featured one wall completely faced with new or reclaimed brick, marble or cedar shingles.

Fireplaces, which were more symbolic than necessary, became simple, faced with brick, rough stone or marble, and reached from floor to ceiling. There were hooded fireplaces, centrally placed in a room, and double-duty fireplaces, designed to serve two rooms and seen from two sides—the dining and living areas.

Doors became flush and some were sliding. Sliding glass double doors opened to the outside. Windows remained traditionally double hung, but casements and jalousies also became popular. Large, expansive windows remained intact and inoperable due to air conditioning. Stairways opened up, with simplified structures of modern design. Oftentimes, they seem to be suspended in space.

It has been said that Frank Lloyd Wright was the inventor of the modern American house, creating the "open plan" by eliminating doors and whole walls. How well I know. I wish I had some of those walls back—to hang things on them, of course.

Furniture related to this period is Gropius, Wright, Van der Rohe, Eames, Risom, Juhl, McCobb, Jacobsen, Laszio and Nelson.

DISTINGUISHING ROOM FEATURES

An empty room consists of four walls, a floor, a ceiling, a door or two and windows. But in miniature, an empty room has three walls; the fourth wall usually becomes a glass front . . . or the appearance of a store front that swings aside.

Finishing off a room becomes a major challenge. Once the miniaturist has settled upon a certain "kind" of room, there are still dozens of decisions to wrestle with. What kind of architectural details and decorations will there be? How will the walls be rendered? Is woodwork to be painted or stained? How will the windows be styled and will there be one, two or three windows? What style of fireplace is suitable (Fig. 3–5)? What will the flooring be like? These are only a few of the questions that the miniaturist will ponder, but time, interest and abundant enthusiasm conquer all. One by one, the pieces fall into place; step by step, a room takes shape, revealing weeks or months of painstaking patience and hard work.

When planning a room, it is always helpful to observe photographs of real-life counterparts. These are readily available in library books, magazines and catalogues. Studying what the professionals have already done can help you determine the styling, structure, coloring and interior design of your future room. Although plain, straight

Fig. 3-4 *Modern Library* (c. 1925) was created by Mrs. Thorne. New ideas emerged and many different combinations of fabric texture, metal and wood became part of a single scene. A square look prevailed among furnishings. Ceilings, wall areas, doorways, window frames and fireplace mantels were tailored and simple. Books, all hand-tooled in silver, grace the two tall bookcases. A patio garden is viewed through the left side window. (*Augustus Beinlich, photograph; courtesy of Phoenix Art Museum*)

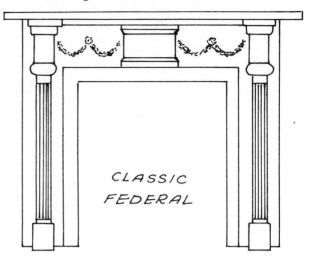

CLASSIC
FEDERAL

DRAWINGS ARE REDUCED IN SIZE

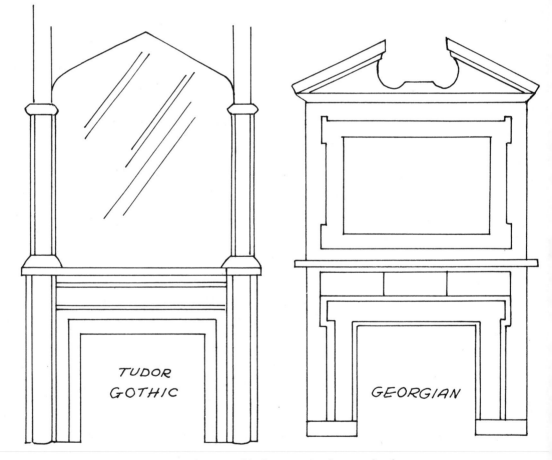

TUDOR
GOTHIC

GEORGIAN

Fig. 3–5 Fireplaces suitable for various architectural styles.

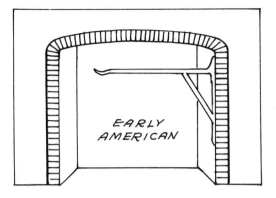

EARLY AMERICAN

DRAWINGS ARE REDUCED IN SIZE

EARLY AMERICAN

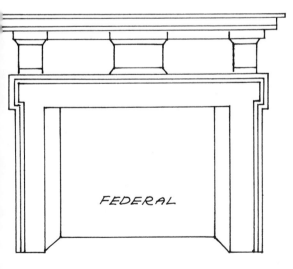

FEDERAL

walls can and do suffice for many miniaturists, it is far more exciting to see innovative features that lift a room from bland to dramatic.

A *two-level floor* has an "uplifting" effect on a room in more ways than one (Fig. 3–6). It can be a small portion in a corner or a whole area along one, two or three walls. The step-up area can be straight or curved, depending upon your ultimate plans. The height of the second level can be one, two or more steps high and a bannister or planters can also become added features along the edges.

Windows

Windows provide an innovative feature *if* they aren't entirely obscured by curtains and drapery. Several examples are shown in Fig. 3–7. There are bay windows (angled or curved) and seat windows. As well as being charming, these provide a three-dimensional effect, adding more depth to a room. French windows which are high and narrow become French doors when extended to the floor. They are hinged to swing outward and can lead out onto a balcony or into a garden. Attractive fanlight windows may be located over doorways or square-head windows, or may retain an individual place in hallways, entrance halls or over built-in bookcases.

The Palladian window is an elegant structure of three windows, with the center window arched at the top; windows on each side are shorter and square-headed. And who can resist the stained glass of a window that sends rays of colored light splashing through a room? Although we don't see many etched windows, that may be a novel approach to a small area. The side windows by entrance doors are often

Fig. 3–6 Eight drawings to provide inspiration for new room settings.

SIDE-LIGHT WINDOWS
BY DOOR

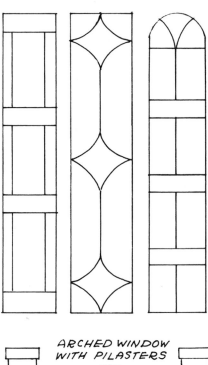

PALLADIAN WINDOW   (REDUCED IN SIZE)

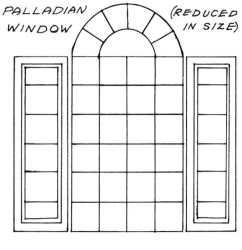

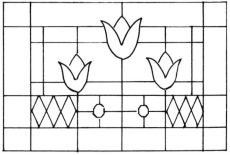

DESIGN FOR STAINED GLASS
TULIPS ARE RED; FILL IN
OWN COLORS; LEAVE SOME
AREAS CLEAR.

ARCHED WINDOW
WITH PILASTERS

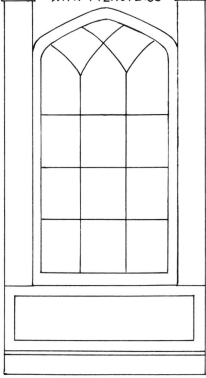

(REDUCED IN SIZE)

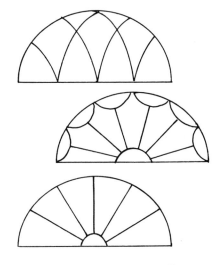

FAN-LIGHT WINDOWS

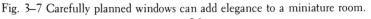

Fig. 3–7 Carefully planned windows can add elegance to a miniature room.

31

designed in unusual and beautiful ways and, lest we forget, there are the simple panes of glass, small squares or diamonds, that have their own special appeal.

Staircases

Staircases reflect gracious living. Truly a functional element, they can be severely plain or dramatically elegant (Fig. 3–8); but no matter which, they should always look safe. Many times a staircase becomes the focal point in a room or setting, taunting the guest to climb to forbidden private areas.

The staircase may or may not have a reason for being in a miniature room, but if you intend to include one, allow a few more inches on the size of your room. If a staircase of full height and stature ascends to the "second" floor, it may or may not have a landing. Some staircases hug the wall and other stairways originate within the room, following a circular pattern or branching off in two different directions. The stairway may require only a few steps leading down to a "sunken" floor or leading up to a balcony. Sometimes a staircase begins within the room and disappears behind a wall—which is an admission of fakery, but it's all very acceptable in miniature.

Balconies, Pillars and Finishing Touches

A *balcony* is a projected platform from a wall, enclosed by a railing. Extend this platform along one wall and notice how much more interesting your room will become. Since balconies are not features that fit every kind of room, this is one that you would use with discretion, but a full two-story room with a balcony could very well be the answer to some sticky problems.

I love *pillars!* They make a room look majestic and dignified and there are numerous ways to show these in a tasteful manner. They enhance an entrance hall (Fig. 3–9), glamorize a balcony and add distinction to a doorway. They can be simple or elaborate, depending upon their use and location. So do use pillars in at least one of your creations.

Remember to include *built-in planters* in some of your arrangements. It's easy enough to place an urn, pot or vase somewhere in a room, but a think-ahead pattern is necessary for the built-in planter, which becomes a permanent interior fixture. The planter can be placed at the front of a box room or worked into some other arrangement.

If you can arrange your room with an *angled wall* or one that juts forward in one or two places, this will also change the perspective of your design (see Fig. 3–6). A part of the room that sticks out adds an aura of mystery. The viewer just can't help wondering what's behind the protruding portion. It may be an empty shell or, for those who wish to wire a room for electricity, the extra space becomes an appropriate area for storing the transformer.

Moldings and Trims

There are marvelous supply sources and dealers who have miniature trims and moldings available; these all provide a realistic touch for finishing off a fine room. But large hardware stores and home care centers unexpectedly produce some beautiful objects from their building sections which can be transformed into the decorative scheme of things. Dowels, spindles, finials, trim moldings and carved trims become useful adjuncts (Fig. 3–10). These may sometimes seem rather heavy by comparison to miniature trim, but when used in proper perspective, they become beautiful structural building material.

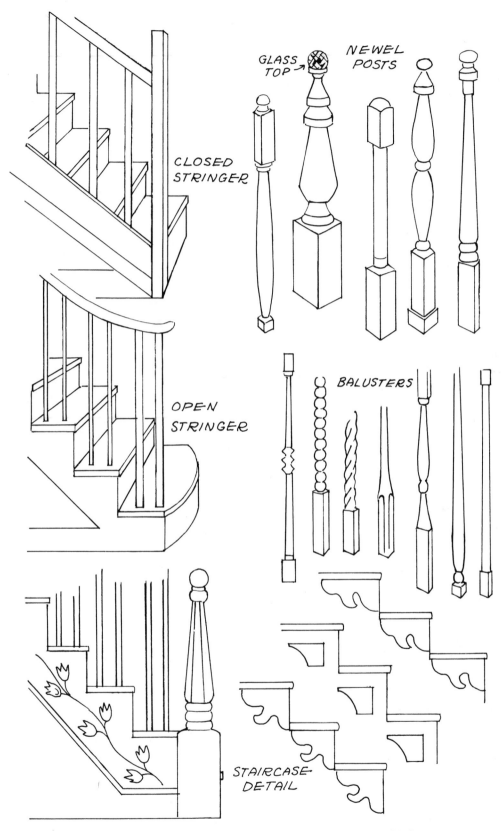

CLOSED STRINGER

GLASS TOP

NEWEL POSTS

OPEN STRINGER

BALUSTERS

STAIRCASE DETAIL

Fig. 3–8 Drawings of open and closed staircases, newel posts and balusters.

33

Fig. 3–9 Pillars become stately features of a finished and furnished room. Two tall white dowels rest on dividers. The stained-glass window is imitation, using a combination of stained glass paint, permanent marking pens and colored tissue paper. Notice that the floor has been scored to simulate planks of wood.

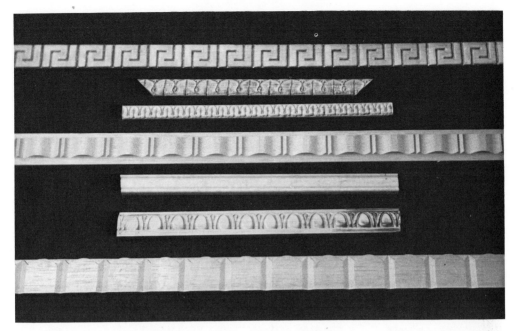

Fig. 3–10 An assortment of carved trim moldings are available in different widths and designs. They prove useful for architectural construction and decoration in a room, for modern furniture construction, and, also, for framing the front of a box or other finishing techniques.

Fig. 3–11 Finials can be used to make beautiful large urns—stained, painted, gilded and decorated. A spindle becomes a pedestal table (see Fig. 10–5).

Fig. 3–12 Embossed wood carvings are available at home care centers. Used imaginatively, these and other selections can prove dramatic, handsome adjuncts in decorating or furniture construction.

Trim molding can become an elegant cove mold and thin moldings can be made into window cornices. Others become attractive mantelpieces and trims around doors and windows.

Finials, in different sizes, can be transformed into urns by turning the hole topside (Fig. 3–11). These can be finished off in a variety of ways.

Embossed decorative wood carvings, such as those in Fig. 3–12, can be imaginatively used as an elegant headboard, a backpiece for a wall fountain, magnificent wall trim in a posh restaurant. Other turned pieces become lamp bases, vases and pedestals for tables.

Yes, there's much to be discovered at your local stores.

CHAPTER

4

Planning and Constructing a Basic Box

MATERIALS SELECTION

I wish I could specify one thickness of wood for all basic boxes and let it go at that, but it's not quite so simple. The way the front is finished off will determine the thickness of wood to be used. For instance, I do appreciate the appearance of a lovely glass or acrylic-framed front and often the frame molding is matched to the styling or type of room involved. An Early American room is set off by a simple, dark-pine frame, while a plush white and gold "fantasy" bedroom is framed in gold Victorian style. Since frames have a rabbet edging which allows for 1/4" insertion, it becomes necessary to use 1/4" plywood which nicely fits within the grooved area.

If a frame is not to be used and sliding sections will instead provide an enclosure, then you can use heavier 3/8" or 1/2" plywood for box construction. Personally, I stay with 1/4" plywood, regardless.

The lumberyard always has a supply of fir and pine plywoods in various thicknesses but a cabinetmaker usually has a broader assortment of plywoods,

including a selection of birch, luan mahogany, walnut and others, depending upon what they're presently working on at the shop. Pine is the least expensive, but the finer woods do provide a nice outer finish with minimum work.

Plywoods do have one better side and it's wise to place it on the *outside*. The inside of the box is usually painted, papered or otherwise covered. Also, if there are knotholes that make you unhappy, do not despair. Plug them up with wood dough or plastic wood (a pliable substance) and, when this has dried, the surface can be sanded smooth.

The strongest box would be made of 1/2" pine, which would naturally be heavy. If the box is intended for a tremendous amount of travel and abuse, this thickness may be necessary, but I believe that miniatures must be treated like valued art. Therefore, I opt for a delicate-looking box.

Bumpers

If you are adding a frame to the front, the bottom of the frame will extend below the box. Therefore, the rest

Fig. 4–1 A ¼″ pine plywood box was constructed for Early American furnishings. The simple frame is secured at the side with a continuous hinge. Note the wood block feet on the bottom of box and tack glides under blocks.

of the box has to be leveled off with bumpers. I have cut thick blocks of pine wood and glued these to the bottom of the box. (See directions for Basic Box.) If the bumpers are foreshortened, tack bumpers or tack glides can also be added and I do favor adding these to the blocks (Fig. 4–2). If blocks are not needed, then bumpers alone can be used.

Adhesive and Nails

There is only one adhesive that I use for constructing a box and that is tried-and-true Liquid Hide Glue, which comes in a convenient plastic bottle, topped with a sensible slit spout for dis-

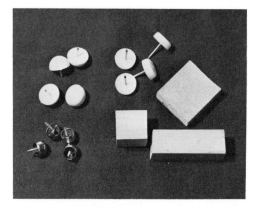

Fig. 4–2 Raising a box above the table surface is sometimes necessary or advisable. The open area under the box provides room for fingers and facilitates lifting. To help with this process are rubber tack bumpers, plastic tack glides, small metal box bumpers and blocks of wood.

pensing the glue. Since this is a really sticky substance, it's advisable to have a damp cloth handy to wipe away any excess amount that drips.

After glue is applied, the box edges are reinforced with nails (¹/₂ 20 GA) or brads (⁵/₈ 19 GA).

FRAMING AND EXTERIOR FINISHING

Boxes can be finished off in different ways. Pine plywood, which has a rather strong pattern, looks quite nice with a dark stain of walnut or jacobean. An additional finish can be obtained by applying a light paint and wiping it off or using one of the antique finishes, applied according to directions.

Mahogany, birch and other fine plywoods are enhanced with a natural sealer and finish of shellac or polyurethane.

Vinyl wall covering makes a good outside cover (Fig. 4–3). Careful selection of a quiet, solid color provides a neat appearing box and the advantage is that vinyl can be easily cleaned. If vinyl is used, the special vinyl paste must be purchased.

Wallpaper also makes a good outer covering and this can be nicely related to the interior in carrying out a special theme. Many wallpapers have a washable surface. Finally, any surface can be spray painted with either flat or glossy finish.

Fig. 4–3 Commercial wallpapers and attractive vinyls can be used to cover the outer surface of a box room when the wood is less than desirable in appearance.

Frames and Sliding Devices

After putting so much effort into your little room you do want to protect it from dust and itchy fingers, so a glass or acrylic front is a must.

The front appearance of a box can be improved by the addition of a frame, using moldings that differ from simple oak to gold baroque. Some miniaturists select one style of molding and use this for all their boxes, maintaining a similar outside look. On the other hand, a frame can be coordinated with the inside of the room, offering a different approach each time.

A basic box can be constructed first and the frame can be made to fit the front *or* I have sometimes switched the method around. Since I'm an addicted frame collector, I sometimes have a suitable frame available and then the basic box is specially built to fit within the frame.

Constructing any frame will require a miter box. Or you can make a trip to your local framer for a job well done. Stock-size frames, finished and unfinished, are also available at paint stores, picture framers, etc. Do-it-yourself-framers shops are springing up, too, and are popular.

Upon completion of the frame, the glass is stapled into place with diamond-shaped studs. This is a glazier's tool.

A simpler method for protecting the front is to use a sliding device (it cannot be locked). Again, there is a choice of construction. One method is to glue a narrow strip of wood (batten) inside both sides of the box about $3/16''$ to $1/4''$ inside the front edges (Fig. 4–4). The *top front* was also cut back $1/4''$ to allow $1/8''$ acrylic to slide down between mold-

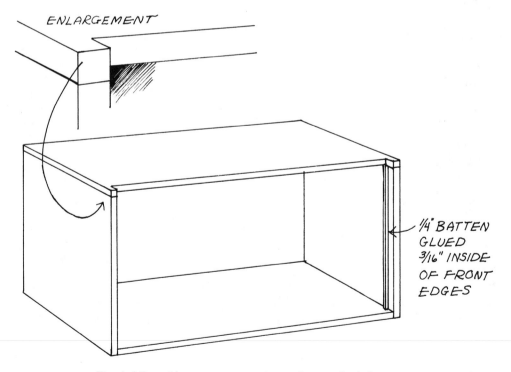

ENLARGEMENT

1/4" BATTEN GLUED 3/16" INSIDE OF FRONT EDGES

Fig. 4–4 Box with cutaway top portion and recessed side battens.

ing and batten. Decorative molding, purchased at the home/hardware store, is fitted, mitered and affixed to the outside as a frame with glue and nails (Fig. 4–5).

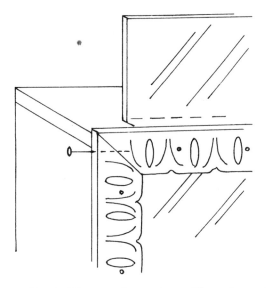

Fig. 4–5 Drawing shows trim molding mitered, fitted and glued onto outside of box. Small nails provide reinforcement; acrylic is measured and cut to fit within slotted area.

I have also purchased the edging used for vinyl panels (molded plastic) and have nailed two strips of this across top and bottom so the acrylic slides from side to side (Fig. 4–6).

Northeastern Scale Models has a strip of grooved wood which I have used, but this will only accommodate a sheet of acrylic that is $1/32''$ thick.

Hinges and Latches

Although some boxes may be permanently closed up, it's not advisable. After all, the glass or acrylic front may need cleaning inside or perhaps you want to do some redecorating. Incidentally, acrylic is cleaned with a light spraying of Pledge and rubbed with a soft furniture cloth.

A glass-framed front can be nicely hinged at the side and this is where my husband is wonderfully cooperative. He accepted the laborious task of hingeing and latching my boxes.

A *piano hinge* or *continuous hinge*

Fig. 4–6 A corner molding used for vinyl wall panels becomes a useful sliding device for an acrylic front. Slotted metal from model hobby shop and slotted wood for $1/16''$ acrylic are alternatives.

Fig. 4–7 A sheet of acrylic neatly slides down between molding trim and box, protecting the contents from dust. If you have a surplus of miniatures with no home, try making an arrangement of collectibles similar to this one.

Fig. 4–8 A piano hinge or continuous hinge is recommended for a door-hung box. Decorative hinges can be used on smaller box rooms where there is less stress. Brass corners are also useful for the permanently enclosed box.

(Fig. 4–8), purchased at a lumber or hardware store, is cut to the necessary length of 11″ and screwed onto frame and side of box. Since the plywood side is ¼″ thick, an additional supportive slice of ¼″ wood is glued to the side *under the hinge* to provide extra strength for the screws. This would not be necessary for thicker boxes.

Latches and *hasps* come in a variety of shapes and sizes and you really have to survey your needs to decide what is most suitable. Some hooks merely flip through a hasp and others are designed to accommodate a padlock. So you have to decide whether you need stringent security. There are both plain and decorative styles, suitable for most any style of construction (Fig. 4–9).

Basic Box Construction

As with any subject, there are differences of opinion regarding the initial step in box construction. One person prefers to finish off the walls first, before joining the sides together, while another box maker will butt and glue the sides and bottom together and then finish the walls. When purchasing a ready-made box, you have no choice and hence no problem. I have tried both procedures and feel neither is more advantageous *unless* a wall is very intricate, such as one with paneling, in which case it is easier to do the wall first. But unlike a dollhouse, a single room can be conveniently turned over on its sides to accommodate wall trimming and decorating; so you must ultimately decide this one for yourself.

But first things first: planning is essential for good results. Assuming that you have first decided on paper where you are placing a see-through window, an open doorway or whatever else you want, then you must decide what is to

Fig. 4–9 Latches and hasps open and close easily. Some are designed to accept a padlock for extra protection.

be cut out of a wall area and what is to remain intact (Fig. 4–10).

Sand all wood surfaces thoroughly. The floor is finished off first with floorboards, marble, terrazzo tile, linoleum, brick or stone. Some of these are simulated. Wall-to-wall carpeting does not have to be put in at this time. It can be measured, cut and glued into place later. Besides, you may still be considering your color scheme.

Inside construction of wall areas is completed with wallpapering or painting, wainscoting, paneling and other trims of your choice. I add baseboards *after* walls are glued and nailed to the floor and add cove molding *after* top is glued and nailed to the walls. Remember to miter your corners on any trims that need it.

Fig. 4–10 Before joining the sides of your box, cut out all openings that are designated for see-through windows or doorways. This is the shell for the needlework shop in Chapter 10.

Glue the parts together, following Fig. 4–11 and the succeeding steps.

1. Apply a thin layer of glue evenly along one side edge of (A) and lowest part of side (B). When tacky, butt together and hammer five brads or nails through both pieces. Space nails evenly, starting at each end. Add third nail in center, making sure the floor is not warping. Add last two nails centered between. If a nail is hammered in crooked, extract immediately and start again.

2. Repeat with other side of (A) and (B).

3. Repeat process with back edge of (A) and back (C), at the same time gluing side edges of (C) and back edges of (B) together. Nail all sections together as done in step 1. For long width, use extra nails. Correct any warpage by bending wood back into place; in fact, you may need an extra pair of hands to assist.

4. Windows are completed separately, using special scale-model window structures, available from dealers or of your own invention. Shades, curtains or draperies are affixed to window and entire unit is positioned and glued.

5. Affix doors in place, complete with paneling, door knobs and added hinges.

6. Extras, such as mantel, hearth, and other wall furnishings, are added.

7. Lighting fixtures are installed and all effects are connected to wires and special units (see Sources of Supply for further information).

8. Inside top is painted with white acrylic paint or papered with white ceiling paper. Wet outside top of box room to prevent warpage.

9. Glue and nail top to walls of box.

10. Finish off outside of box, following suggestions in the preceding section.

11. Complete room furnishings and

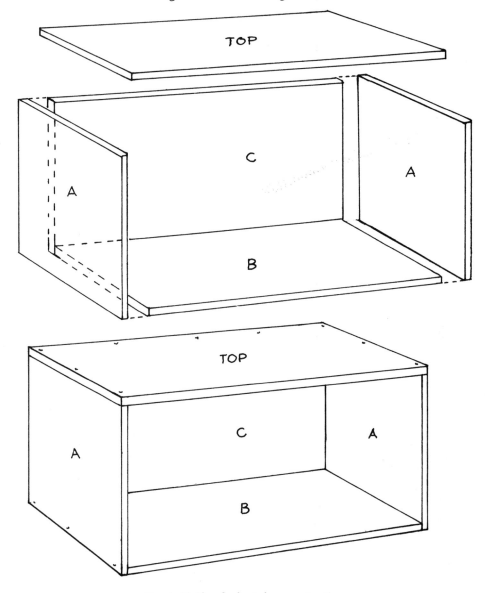

Fig. 4–11 Plan for basic box construction.

adhere everything in place with wax Stickum.

SIMULATED SURFACE FINISHES
Scoring

Sometimes, due to a lack of certain supplies on hand, I've had to be innovative when finishing off a project and that's when I resort to scoring. Scoring is a method of indenting lines on a variety of surfaces with a pointed tool. Scoring is most effective for acquiring a series of straight lines, usually evenly spaced, which may end up as wainscoting or even as an entire floor. There are a few items in room construction that can be imitated with this useful method and it's less costly and time consuming than the more authentic replicas.

Scoring is accomplished by pulling a

pointed instrument along the side of a metal-edge ruler or T square, which is placed on top of the surface to be scored. Some points work better on different surfaces.

> Hardwood requires a sharp instrument; for pine, oak, etc., use the point of a compass or large drapery hook
>
> Soft balsa wood requires a blunt tip, such as a used ballpoint pen or small stylus
>
> Illustration board requires a cutting point; use compass point, large drapery hook
>
> Use a blunt instrument for sandpaper

A plain plywood floor can be made by planning your scored lines about ¼″ apart. Measure and mark your areas regularly so your lines remain straight. Score with the grain of wood. Use a natural stain finish or polyurethane.

Remember, if you do score a floor, this is done *before* you assemble a box.

Wainscoting can be scored on strips of balsa wood, 3″ x ¹/₃₂″ thick. Several of these strips are cut to necessary height (about 2½″ to 3″ high), allowing enough for area needed (Fig. 4–12). Strips are *very lightly* scored in the direction of grain and glued into place along lower part of wall, resting on floor. Wainscoting is stained light or dark, or painted. A chair rail (stained or painted) is added to top.

A second method for wainscoting is cutting sections of illustration board for the wall area and scoring these with a sharp-pointed object. After the cardboard wainscoting is glued to the wall and thoroughly dry, it is painted with an acrylic paint and white glue mixture, which hardens the board and preserves

Fig. 4–12 An example of scoring is the balsa-wood wainscoted area of this box, the beginning of an Early American room. The baseboards are strips of ¹/₃₂″ balsa, lightly scored near top and sanded round.

it. Painted white, it looks very effective in a kitchen and pantry area.

Baseboards are easily simulated (see Fig. 4–12). Cut strips of $1/16''$-thick balsa wood to $1/2''$-wide strips. Long cut is with the grain. Measure and cut to fit room. Score one line along strips about $1/16''$ down from top of baseboard. Sand top of baseboard, rounding the edge; paint white, tan or color of your choice. Glue baseboard into position on wall. Glue on small quarter-round strips to finish off where baseboard meets floor, if you prefer to finish it off this way.

Additional uses for scoring could include brick patterns, molding designs and marble sectioning.

Texture Imitation

Simulation, which is the imitation or reasonable facsimile of a surface or object, can be a useful, time-saving and economical procedure. Although there are exquisite wooden parquet floors, real marble, tiny minibricks and much, much more actually available to the miniaturist, it is sometimes feasible to "make do" or attempt a near-accurate copy, depending upon your personal needs and financial resources.

Parquetry (wooden mosaic) or *marquetry* (inlaid work of wood) is achieved by painting on the wood with different stain colors. To prevent the stain from bleeding, a *tiny* amount of white glue is added to the stain, which is poured into a small lid cover. If stain is gooey, then too much glue has been added. Experiment. Each application of different stain should be allowed to dry before next color stain is applied (see Belle of Amherst parquet box in Ch. 11).

Marble can be achieved with Contact paper, vinyl floor tile, Amtico Renaissance pattern tile, Formica or Marlite.

Wood floors can be simulated with special miniature paper of wood designs; Contact paper; scoring the surface of plywood, using a metal-edge ruler and blunt instrument (see previous section); Popsicle sticks.

Brick is made from medium-grade sandpaper, painted red and scored with a blunt instrument; or sandpaper is cut into brick sizes and glued onto area to be covered.

Linoleum can be duplicated with vinyl tile, wallpaper pattern finished with polyurethane varnish or shellac, oilcloth, Contact paper, plastic placemats.

Construction and Design Simulation

Iron work can be created from heavy lace trims painted black and stiffened with diluted white glue or from plastic produce baskets painted with PLA black enamel (Fig. 4–13).

Stained glass is made by using special glass stain paint; permanent marking pens (Sharpie); gluing cutouts of colored tissue paper to surface.

Stairway designs can be made with gold embossed paper, painted white.

Stairway supports can be "iron work" described above (see Fig. 4–13).

Cane used in furniture construction is needlepoint canvas (12–14 mesh), painted with tan acrylic and stiffened with white glue.

Glass is acrylic sheet, $1/16''$ or $1/8''$ thick.

Glass bowls can be made in different sizes and designs by using plastic Shrink Art, purchased at a craft store (Fig. 4–14).

Pottery is made from cutout portions of papier mâché egg cartons, hardened with white glue and painted (Fig. 4–15).

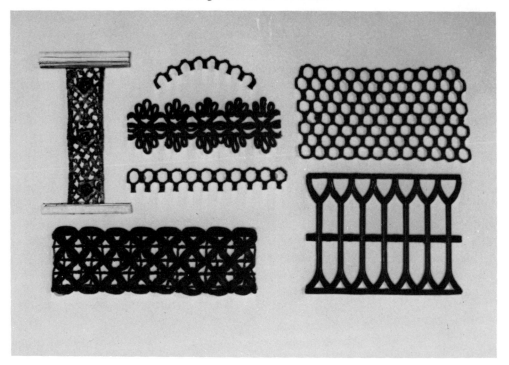

Fig. 4–13 Iron work designs are devised from lace trim, gilt edging, honeycomb plastic pot scrubber, rayon ribbon trim and plastic produce container. All are painted black and stiffened with white glue.

Fig. 4–14 Glass bowls of various designs and sizes are acquired by placing different-size buttons on varying cutout shapes (squares, circles, ovals) of Shrink Art plastic, which is baked in the oven. Finished bowls are in white saucer.

Fig. 4–15 Pottery containers, such as bowls, platters, vases and planters, are contrived from cutout portions of papier mâché egg cartons. They are colored and stiffened with white glue and paint mixture. Tiny designs are added.

Lighting fixtures are made from pieces of jewelry and findings.

Some *foods* or other objects can be made from seeds of fruit: peaches from cherry pits; cherries from grape pits; platters from half-split plum pits; leaves from dried squash seeds; plant structure from dried grape twigs, after the grapes have been eaten.

Napkin Ring Creations

What do you see when you look at a napkin ring? Is it merely an aperture waiting to hold a napkin? Take another glance because it can be much more than that to the miniaturist.

Available in wood, metal, glass, ceramic, plastic, bone, leather, papier mâché, fabric, they end up with a variety of styles and holes. No longer is the napkin ring just a "ring" in shape. Triangles, ovals, squares and oblongs are also popular.

Several ideas are shown in Fig. 4–16. Wide holders with a depth of an inch or more can become pedestals for cocktail tables and foundations for hassocks. Or they can become beautiful plant holders, either left in their singular state or mounted on top of something else . . . perhaps an egg stand. Delicate narrow holders can become frames for

Fig. 4–16 Napkin holders are quite varied in design and composition. They can end up as planters, hassocks, containers, frames, shadowboxes, wall units and anything else your imagination can provoke.

objects or trays, and medium-size ones become shadowbox frames or wall shelves. Several placed together as wall units will store the soft goods of commercial products. Often two, three, or four can be glued together for some special reason or wooden designs can be cut in half, quartered or sliced, which opens up a few more unique possibilities. Yes, take a second look at napkin rings and ponder their usefulness in a miniature way.

CHAPTER

5

Personalized Rooms, Shadowboxes and Vignettes

An heirloom is an heirloom, but one that is *personalized* becomes so much more meaningful. It doesn't take extraordinary inspiration to create one of these little gems. Day in and day out, your calendar probably reminds you of an upcoming birthday, anniversary, graduation or some other special day to honor. Perhaps you want to remember happy holidays spent with family or friends. Or you may wish to immortalize your own family in miniature.

PERSONALIZING FAMILY VIGNETTES

Big or small, solidify a *family* in miniature. It's not necessary to include dolls in your little scene; in fact, I sometimes think that the doll figure can detract from the rest of the items. A family room can be shown with favorite pieces of furniture, surrounded by personal items related to work, play, study or whatever else makes your loved ones function happily. Also, a 2"-deep dimensional box with cubbyholes can complete the concept of a family and my own is offered as a suggestion. Family memorabilia can be miniaturized and fitted into a printer's type box or you can construct several vignette rooms and attach them together when finished. How exciting it would be to see a long section of individual family remembrances running along a wall and, if the family enlarges, then just add on another room. Don't forget to include the family pet . . . woof! woof! . . . meow! meow! . . . squeak? squeak?

I purchased the subdivided wooden structure shown in Fig. 5–1 as the first step in my personalized family heirloom. Using Hermes paper for two rooms, the walls were appropriately papered for each member of the family. The frame in Fig. 5–2 was then prepared, including the shadowbox, to accommodate the depth of the vignette structure. The outside of the shadowbox was stained and the inside covered with upholstery material, glued into place with Velverette. Velvet ribbon was applied to the four side areas of the inside.

Miniatures were made or contrived to finish off each cubbyhole with characteristic articles of personal interest (Fig. 5–3). Since my plant room houses corn plants that tower 8' and 12' high, the little room at upper left has to have one, too. Other little items are palette,

Fig. 5–1 A unique, subdivided shadowbox from Heirloom Crafts resembles a house. Since the height of vignette rooms is scant, miniatures have to be scaled ¹/₂″ to 1′. Other structures of this type, available at crafts stores, have a lesser or greater number of rooms.

seashells, watercolor painting, fabrics for sewing, shopping bag (designer) and boxes, boxes, boxes for stowing all my junk.

My husband, a busy physician (medical bag), wears three other hats as a deputy fire chief, active county deputy fire coordinator and a major in the Civil Air Patrol. He flies a twin Apache and has several hobbies, all depicted. The small fish tank is made this time from a Tic-Tac dispenser. Our son, the

Fig. 5–2 An attractive frame of gold and imitation tortoise is selected to accommodate the size, including extra area, of the vignette structure in Fig. 5–1. The shadowbox in foreground is constructed of ⅛″ plywood to accommodate the depth of the vignette structure and to fit within the frame (see Fig. 5–5).

medical student (skull), is Miami based (banner) and his other interests of skiing, scuba diving and karate are represented. Also shown is his passion for chocolate (a candy bar) and an overflowing trash basket for untidiness, what else?

Our cat, Furry, shows off his essentials, but boasts most about his mouse trophy (pussy willow) and portraits of his lady love mounted on the wall. Each cubicle also has an appropriate calendar with birthday noted. The peaked attic area stores the interesting memorabilia of past hobbies and occasions. This really could have been stuffed with far more than is shown.

Birthdays can be very special. Sweet sixteen, the magic age of twenty-one, "life begins at forty" or the half-century mark are all themes which can be dealt with imaginatively. But then, no special year really matters. Any birthdate and any miniature creation would be happily welcomed by any birthday "boy or girl." No matter what age, there's always a generous number of personal goods and designated achievements to dignify a room or box.

If you have an *anniversary* to commemorate, there are twice as many personal features for inspiration. Create an actual room with the celebrating couple watching television, playing cards, read-

Fig. 5–3 The miniaturized family heirloom is complete, with a number of the hobbies and interests of each member of the family displayed.

ing, cleaning, dancing (to the waltz of a built-in music box), kissing or lounging on a sofa.

Instead of a full-scale anniversary room, you can also make a wall arrangement of personal items, such as the one in Fig. 5–4. This is often more convenient when you're unfamiliar

with the furnishings of a room. The vignette in Fig. 5–4 was made for a very special couple celebrating a twenty-fifth anniversary. The wall is complete with memorabilia, hobbies and incidentals that eloquently depict their interests and life. The decoupaged family photo dominates the wall and an avid love for

Fig. 5–4 This 2"-deep vignette is composed within an 8" x 10" reverse-scoop frame. It is the beginning of a wall arrangement of memorabilia for a very special couple celebrating a twenty-fifth wedding anniversary.

flowers is depicted in the table grouping and the dried pressed-flower arrangement.

The skirted table, the Federal chair and the pitcher and bowl set imitate their own furnishings and their fondness for antiques. The tiny photo bulb is for the photography hobby and the itsy-bitsy baby doll sitting in the pitcher "cries" obstetrician. A hospital volunteer pin speaks of thousands of hours of devoted service. The Mozart record album resting on the chair does double duty since the family both enjoys music and has also produced accomplished pianists. Navy insignia,

Syracuse University banner and a small pipe tell their stories, too. Of course, they do have a cat playing with some yarn. The sterling silver twenty-fifth anniversary disc sums it all up. Happy Anniversary to the Brandons!

Personal contents for such a gift can be handmade or purchased; the size can range from 1" scale down to an even smaller scale if you so desire. Small charms from jewelry stores make nice little minis to "symbolize" the world of your special person, but I suppose greater satisfaction emerges when you make the items in your own inimitable way.

55

The *holiday* theme has been done, but if you copy your own room in miniature and duplicate those special holiday decorations that you've grown so fond of, then you've achieved the personal touch. Recreate your own room enveloped in Christmas cheer or your dining room ready for a dignified Passover service. There's always a New Year's Eve party to remember and who says you have to have a lot of people (dolls) in the room? Just depict it as the morning after with all the confetti, hats, horns, glasses and debris lying around. Well, you might have one doll slumped in a chair or "sleeping it off" on the sofa. Thanksgiving makes a festive holiday and allows you to give full vent to a delicious repast. Halloween, Easter, Chanukah, St. Patrick's Day or any of the great remembered times can be different and challenging for a box full of treasured memories.

And then there's *graduation!* High school, training school, college or professional school can offer marvelous possibilities. Even insignificant items and experiences become especially important during youthful years. Miniature memories can stretch back through childhood, clutching at dreams and laughing at errors. The past is all caught up in that one magic moment of graduation and once again the creative miniaturist can pull it together with tiny objects, meaningful achievements, thoughts and loves of yesteryear.

Have some guaranteed fun! Create a miniature of personal nature.

Making Framed Shadowboxes

There are many commercial frames readily available for use. Moldings vary from thin to wide and from rough primitive to ornate. Scoops or curved areas may thrust forward or be reversed. Because the molding stretches back toward the wall, the reverse scoop is my favorite style for a box vignette.

Taking advantage of the manufactured frame, the miniaturist can select his or her own size and proceed to construct a simple box. Whether the box ends up horizontal or vertical in use depends upon your own preference, but requires careful planning.

A very comfortable size is 8″ x 10″, which will be described for the benefit of the reader. So gather together some balsa wood and glue and you'll be on your way to creating and decorating your own shadowbox or vignette.

MATERIALS

8″ x 10″ reverse scoop frame; 8″ x 10″ glass; 8″ x 10″ cardboard, 1/8″ thick; balsa wood, 2″ wide x 1/4″ thick; craft glue; wallpaper, fabric or wood veneer for background.

DIRECTIONS

1. Cut balsa wood to sizes indicated at (A) in Fig. 5–5.

2. Glue your selection of wall covering to 8″ x 10″ cardboard and to two side areas of balsa wood. Extend material around to cover 1/4″ sides, too. Allow to dry.

3. Finish off bottom piece of balsa wood with carpet or other finish of your choice. If carpeting is used, extend material over onto both 1/8″ sides.

4. Assemble the four sections of balsa wood as indicated in drawing (B). Test for fit into frame. If satisfied, remove from frame and glue four sides together.

5. When four sides are secure, glue background piece onto back of balsa wood edges.

6. Add a baseboard molding (stained or painted) to back wall and side areas. Be sure to miter corners so they fit well together.

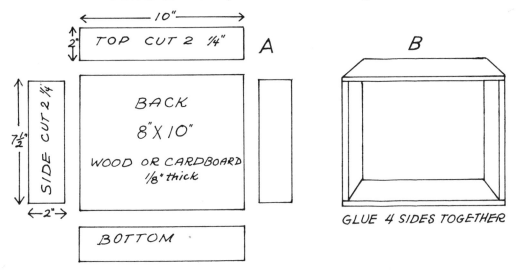

Fig. 5–5 Pattern and assembly guide for the basic framed shadowbox.

7. Now you're on your own to complete the wall arrangement. Secure everything well with craft glue or Stickum for small pieces.

8. With a bit of glue, place clean glass in position in frame.

9. Put some craft glue along inner areas of frame and place your five-sided finished piece securely into position next to glass.

10. Hammer tiny $^3/8''$ nails through the back of cardboard into balsa wood at

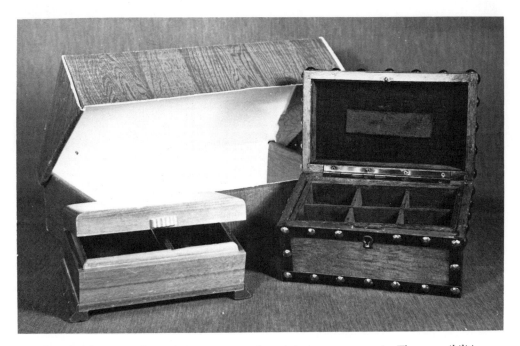

Fig. 5–6 Boxes can become unique rooms for miniature arrangements. Three possibilities shown are a fold-up cheese box, a walnut music box and a jewelry box.

Fig. 5–7 A very small area requires a scale of ¹/₄″ to 1′. Tiny plastic sofa and chairs have added fabric; the cocktail table is an etched ring with acrylic round top; tiny pillows are on the sofa. Accessories are the usual bead "vase" and small dried plant life; "candles" of small cut nails, painted white; basket and frames are of links, filigree and wire; ceiling light is a pearl in a bead cap. The tiniest miniatures are *so* precious.

the corners and other areas along edge.

11. Balsa wood sides can be stained, painted or covered with a plain or decorative heavy paper. Wide decorative tape would also make a beautiful side finish.

12. When you add picture hooks for hanging, screw the hooks into the frame molding, *not* into the balsa wood.

Balsa wood is very firm for its weight and, if handled like any valued piece of art, it will hold up very well.

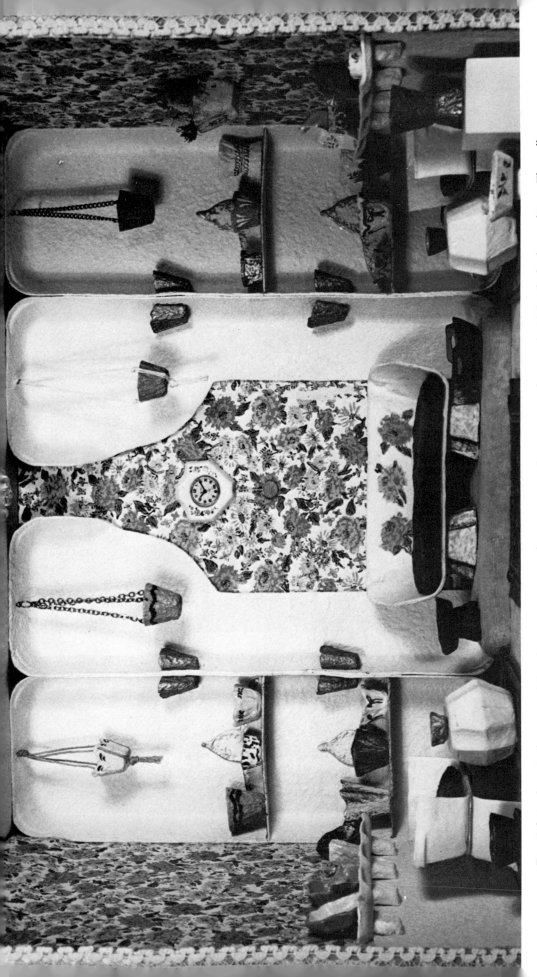

Fig. 5–8 A glamorized corrugated box becomes a pottery showroom. Vases, pots, urns, planters, trays, bowls, are all made from bits and pieces cut from papier mâché egg cartons. Other "architectural" details are made from the covers and flaps of long egg cartons. The settees are made from produce cartons and accented with brushed velvet cushions. The walls are covered with commercial wallpaper and floors are carpeted with pale blue velvet.

Fig. 5–9 A close-up of right side of pottery showroom illustrates the variety of designs and shapes that egg cartons, cuticle scissors and inventiveness can produce. A little white glue and paint mixture is used for finishing touches.

Using Unused Boxes

Everyone makes some purchase that involves a box-constructed object suitable for a miniature display. For an indefinite period of time one claims enjoyment from its use, then for one reason or another it is abandoned.

These lonesome boxes can be reclaimed and glamorized by adding miniature scenes or rooms within their walled areas.

I have a simple walnut *music box* which was once used for cigarettes. Since I no longer condoned smoking, the box had been squashed back into a

Fig. 5–10 Any little girl would love this room, transformed from a used cheese box. The wall covering is fabric and the floor covering is vinyl plastic that resembles linoleum. The sofabed and tricornered pillows are covered in blue dotted swiss. Childhood toys and accessories complete the room.

corner and mostly forgotten. Once in a while I would pull it out, lift up the cover and listen to a lovely, unfamiliar melody.

Today, the box has a new identity: within its tiny square structure is a very tiny room (Figs. 5–6, and 5–7). Now when I open the box, there is not only a pretty tune, but a darling miniature creation. What kind of box do you have around that's been forgotten, neglected and gathering dust?

Jewelry boxes come in assorted styles and sizes. One small, well-constructed box, 5¹/₂″ x 8″, was begging to be used. Since there was a sectional removable tray, I had to decide whether to discard the tray and, using the entire depth of

2³/₄″, construct a wee room or keep the tray and make a vignette room which allowed a depth of 1¹/₂″. I decided to retain the tray and use the sectional areas to display individual miniatures that are handmade and of which I am most fond. The six small sections could also have become teeny-tiny vignette rooms, if one so desired. The lower portion of the box was then finished off, complete with wall covering and itsy-bitsy furnishings.

Corrugated boxes are everywhere and these surely come in various sizes. But I've discovered that there are also variable strengths and thicknesses. Naturally, the stronger box is the solution since this will hold up better over the

Fig. 5–12 When Deborah Murray Couch looked at a file box, she saw great possibilities for a miniature arrangement. Innovatively, she turned this one into three rooms, scaling everything $1/2''$ to $1'$. A cornhusk doll takes care of kitchen duties.

Fig. 5–11 A charming knickknack box measuring 17" high and 2" deep becomes another solution for displaying miniatures. A red velour background sets off three different arrangements, which are mostly made from scratch or from findings.

years. One suggestion is to observe if the box has a double stripping of corrugated edging instead of the usual single stripping. The double is much sturdier. What you intend to include in your box will, of course, influence your size selection. If necessary, a box can be cut down on one side and the cutaway side can be closed up again by joining a section with strong tape and white glue. When it is thoroughly dry, you can proceed to cover or decorate the walls and outside.

Whatever does one do with a *cheese box?* It's well built, strong and has a convenient lift-up cover. For one thing, it can be turned into a small fold-up room (Fig. 5–10). And, while this may not win any great awards for miniature creativity, it can become the most adorable miniature playroom for a young girl to carry with her wherever she may go. Background pieces are securely glued in place so they don't rattle around. Additional small items can be contained in a bag so that arranging and rearranging can be accomplished by its little owner.

Anyone who visits the boutique and gift departments is well aware of the assortment of little *knickknack boxes* that are always available. Oftentimes their design and odd size can be the solution to a problem spot on a wall and, if you're looking for a new and novel way to fill that little box, then miniatures could very well be the answer.

Other boxes which are available and useful are a cigar box, shoebox, pocketbook box, milk carton, Lucite box, sewing box, matchbox, file box, recipe box, hatbox, stationery box.

PART II

Rooms by the Author

If you want to do something well, do it slowly.
. . . . Improve yourself gradually, and do not
lose patience. . . . Develop all your talents,
and each will open for you an exciting new
world. . . . Be as many-sided as you can.
             BALTASAR GRACIÁN (1601–1658)
                        and
             OTTO EISENSCHIML (1880–1963)

Introduction

Like soap bubbles, miniature rooms begin to multiply and, all too soon, one has rooms on top of rooms. That's when I begin to make flat rooftops instead of sloping roofs. But, variety being the spice of life, the novelty of diversified miniatures has rubbed off on me and several favorite rooms are depicted in this section. All were executed by your author and 95 percent of the furnishings are personally created and handmade. The other 5 percent includes the much-admired or needed piece that is purchased, as are some necessary accessories of glass, ceramic, copper, etc. Many items are made from scratch and others are conceived from found materials. Some of the furnishings are described with drawings and directions. Space and time limitations make it impossible to give directions for every piece shown.

Someone asked if I *planned* my interiors, along with arrangement of furnishings, or if everything were casually placed, unplanned, as I went along. I have done both! But to plan a room on paper first is surely more thoughtful and often more appropriate. Determining ahead of time where a piece of furniture will go can influence placement of a window, or vice versa. The position of a fireplace can vary from being centered on a wall, nestled in a corner or even placed in the middle of the room, as in modern structures. Built-in bookcases and cabinets are "think-ahead" projects. Wainscoting may or may not be considered and other architectural details are best preplanned to avoid a collision course with your furnishings. Sometimes, an innovative thought will suddenly pop into your mind during construction, and this is all to the good, for it's the spontaneous idea that helps add "juice" to your working program.

The rooms discussed in this section are not necessarily meant to be exactly copied, but they can prove beneficial in getting the miniaturist started. Any arrangement of architectural detail may suggest other areas or ideas that the reader may wish to incorporate. Often, a selection of furniture or accessory may prove useful in some other room, shop or whatever you may be involved in creating.

So, search within each room setting and reap small benefits in unexpected ways, thus helping you gain insight and inspiration.

CHAPTER
6

Artist's Studio

Before I created the Artist's Studio, there were the usual number of queries from interested people who asked "Why don't you make a miniature studio?" For me, it was the most obvious room to do, so one might say that the studio was created in self-defense.

I was inspired to begin when I luckily came across a darling nude bisque doll which unhesitatingly became my model (Fig. 6–1 and color Fig. 13). All signals were "go" and three months later the studio became a reality.

For someone like me who works out of a basement, this might well represent a fantasy room. But next time, I would probably opt for a studio twice as large because many sacrifices had to be made, due to limited space.

The first decision concerned a box that would clearly show the room, plus the skylight in the roof. Hence a sloping roof was the answer. Essentially, this is a basic box with the front portion higher than the back.

How to Make and Finish a Studio Box

The base of the box is $^3/_8$"-thick plywood and the sides, back and top are $^1/_4$"-thick plywood. A window area of 2" x $3^1/_2$" is cut out of the back and a skylight area of $4^1/_2$" x 6" is cut out of the top. Acrylic is used for "glass" for the back window, but the skylight uses a frosted crackle glass, purchased from a glass dealer. Both windows are finished off with Northeastern window trim and moldings.

Floor and Walls

The floor in this box was laid after the box was built. I purchased a package of commercial parquet flooring which featured wooden strips of 1"-wide planks. There are nine squares in a package. Each square is 12" x 12" and has four sections, held together with wires. The wires are pulled apart. Edges are sawed and sanded smooth and laid down onto plywood base so that "wood planks" run in the same direction. When satisfied with layout, flooring is glued into place. It is weighted down to dry overnight. Liquid Hide Glue is used, but remember that water-based glue will cause warpage. Therefore, plywood must be moistened.

Place masking tape along floor edges. Paint walls, ceiling and trim the color

Fig. 6–1 In one small space, the artist has all the necessities of reclines on a model stand while the artist puts the finishing his trade, plus the conveniences of the good life. A bisque doll touches to a painting.

Fig. 6–2 After floor has been laid down, the rear balcony structure is planned and set in. Window is finished off with casing and sill.

of your choice. I used beige acrylic, already mixed in a jar. Premixed paint is more desirable than mixing your own color from tube paint because touchups may be necessary later on.

Balcony

Proceed to build structure for balcony, which is 1¼″ high. The left side is 4″ deep and the right side is 6″ deep. (Fig. 6–2). Balsa or basswood strips are used. After the outside wall is glued in place, add several strips of thin wood across the open area, gluing *even* with the top. Add a pair of purchased steps or make your own.

Measure and cut a paper floor pattern to fit over open area. When satisfied, transfer pattern onto illustration board and cut it out. Find a wallpaper, or whatever, that resembles linoleum and glue onto illustration-board floor. Glue linoleum floor snugly against wall and onto support strips. Allow to dry thoroughly. Paint linoleum surface with polyurethane gloss or shellac.

Measure and cut baseboards (Northeastern) for both levels of floor. Paint same color as wall and glue into place along sides and back wall.

On paper, determine the design and positioning of the railing, posts and newel posts. Cut out the pieces and complete the carving (see Fig. 3–8). When satisfied, tape waxed paper to graph paper and tape both to board. Place and glue shaped newel posts (carved from ½″ strips of balsa wood), squared posts and banister (Northeastern) on top of waxed paper, using graph paper as a guide for squared angles. When both structures are thoroughly

Fig. 6–3 Linoleum floor is added to balcony. Rails and posts are glued into position as one structure. Stairs are glued into place; lightweight buckram shade is placed in window; skylight and moldings are glued into place and light fixtures added. Ceiling or top is *not* affixed in place until later.

dry, paint them the same color as walls. When dry, glue in position (Fig. 6–3).

Interior and Exterior Details

Make a window shade out of lightweight buckram. Roll up, glue around an applicator stick, add drawpull and glue into window area.

Finish off steps and stain.

Finish off skylight with window strips (inside and outside) and add two hanging light fixtures from ceiling. These are cut from the tops of toothpaste tubes and are wired for electricity.

Since the front of the box will have a sheet of $1/16''$ acrylic (to be measured and cut to fit later), a long piece of slotted basswood (Northeastern) is glued to the upright left and right sides of box. This accommodates acrylic of $1/16''$

thickness only. Dollhouse moldings are added to finish off front areas of sides and bottom.

The outside and back of box are finished at your discretion. I purchased a roll of blue vinyl wall covering in preference to painting or staining. It's durable, colorful and easy to clean. If you do decide to use vinyl, remember to purchase the special adhesive for vinyl wall covering.

Measuring the acrylic for sliding into slotted areas takes care. First measure and cut stiff cardboard, running this up and down for fit. Adjust if necessary, but sometimes it is best to reserve final fit until after roof has been glued down, making sure left and right sides are straight. When cardboard pattern fits appropriately, cut acrylic to this size.

Fig. 6–4 An artist's studio features unusual furnishings and accessories. A work table holds essentials, while a painting on lightweight buckram rests on the studio easel. The drawing table is complete with pastels, permanent lamp and drawing supplies. The tabouret holds other art supplies and the balloon-back chair is an extra piece of furnishing that the little artist probably picked up at an auction. Directions are given in this chapter for all furniture and art supplies shown.

After inside furnishings and accessories are completed, the top is glued down. The roof is finished off with cut rectangles of tan sandpaper, laid over each other to simulate shingles. After top is permanently adhered, quarter round and cove moldings of $1/16''$ (Northeastern) are glued into wall and ceiling corners.

Accessories are glued onto appropriate furnishings, which are either glued down or held in place with wax Stickum.

Interior Furnishings

Deciding what to put in the interior is determined by the tastes of the creator. Since our model initiated this whole affair, she is deservedly immor-

talized on "canvas" made of lightweight buckram glued over balsa-wood stretcher strips. Various works of art—watercolors, portrait sketches, pen and ink drawings—and a bulletin board adorn the walls. Furnishings on the balcony include an unmade cot, cabinet, bookcase, drawing table, stool and tabouret (a cabinet for art supplies). In the foreground are the model stand, a balloon-back chair, studio easel, worktable, rack for paper supplies and canvasses and sink.

All furnishings, which are made from scratch, are covered or filled with the accessories necessary to make our artist's life both pleasant and efficient. The coffee pot, fruit, grocery bag, books, and plant fill some inner needs. The artist is necessarily surrounded by art essentials, all made from scratch or scrap. The pastel set (ends of colored pencils), T square, triangle, ruler, pencil sharpener, brush/water container, spray can, paint jars and tubes, paintbrushes, pencils, sandpad, ink bottles, spatulas, palette, brayer, thumbtacks, scissors, duster brush, eraser, sponges, turpentine cans are all devised from discarded bits of dowel, wood, plastic, metal, hair, and other odds and ends. A diverse assortment of pads, booklets, papers, colored cardboards, canvas and frames rounds out the art materials. Cleaning equipment around the sink consists of deep trays, soap, sponges, towel, broom, dustpan and rags. The dustpan is made from the pulloff tab of cheese containers, and the best bristles for making a broom are from a cobweb broom. They are flexible and fine. If you haven't already guessed, the model's robe over the banister is see-through black lace.

The floor of the studio is immaculately clean, which is unheard of in art circles . . . so, when anyone comments on this, I nonchalantly retort, "Our artist just moved into his new studio last week."

How to Make a Studio Easel

Pattern parts and assembly guide for the easel are shown in Fig. 6–5.

MATERIALS

Sheets of wood (pine or basswood), $1/16''$ and $1/8''$; structural shape H columns, $1/8''$ (Northeastern Scale Models, Inc.); oak stain.

DIRECTIONS

When gluing, all units must be well dried before proceeding to next step.

1. Sand sheets of wood with the grain.

2. Using tracing paper, transfer pattern parts in Fig. 6–5 to wood and cut out shapes. Sand edges. Stain wood.

3. Glue uprights (D) into position against bases (A). Use graph paper (beneath waxed paper) to help line up squared angles.

4. Glue pieces (I), (J) and (K) together for tray. Gently cut away portions of H structure to an L shape as shown in Fig. 6–5. Glue atop (I). Set aside.

5. Glue pieces (B) and (C) into position.

6. Cut another H structure into L shape and glue to piece (L) for "clamp." Set aside. This is placed last to hold top of a canvas in place.

7. Glue pieces (E) and (F) into position.

8. Glue center upright (G) onto (F) and also glue tray to bottom of (G) and onto outside uprights (D). This is not a movable tray so, if your painting is small, you may want to lift the tray higher. Use your own discretion.

9. Glue back piece (H) against crossbar (F) and onto lower back crossbar (C). Top of (H) will need beveling.

10. Place top clamp where needed to hold canvas and glue in place.

11. Shellac the entire easel.

How to Make a Drawing Table

Fig. 6–6 provides pattern parts and assembly sequence for the studio drawing table.

MATERIALS

Pine wood, $1/32''$, $1/16''$, $1/8''$; aluminum from "frozen dinner" plate; $4''$ of 18-gauge copper wire; four screw knobs from earring findings (one knob is larger).

DIRECTIONS

1. Glue front and back legs (E) to upright piece (D). Repeat for other side. Follow side view in Fig. 6–6 for place-

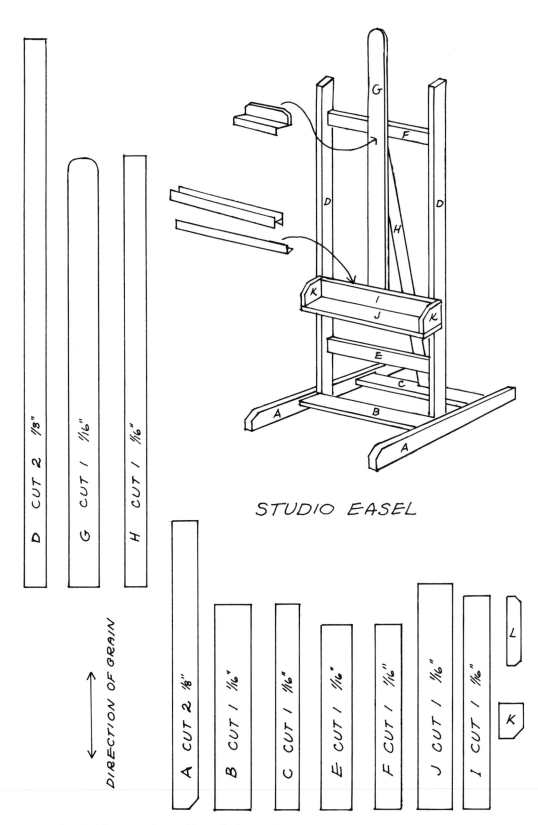

STUDIO EASEL

D CUT 2 ⅛"

G CUT 1 ⁹⁄₁₆"

H CUT 1 ⁹⁄₁₆"

DIRECTION OF GRAIN

A CUT 2 ⅛"

B CUT 1 ⁹⁄₁₆"

C CUT 1 ⁹⁄₁₆"

E CUT 1 ⁹⁄₁₆"

F CUT 1 ⁹⁄₁₆"

J CUT 1 ⁹⁄₁₆"

I CUT 1 ⁹⁄₁₆"

L

K

Fig. 6–5 Pattern and assembly guide for a studio easel, made from pine and stained dark.

74

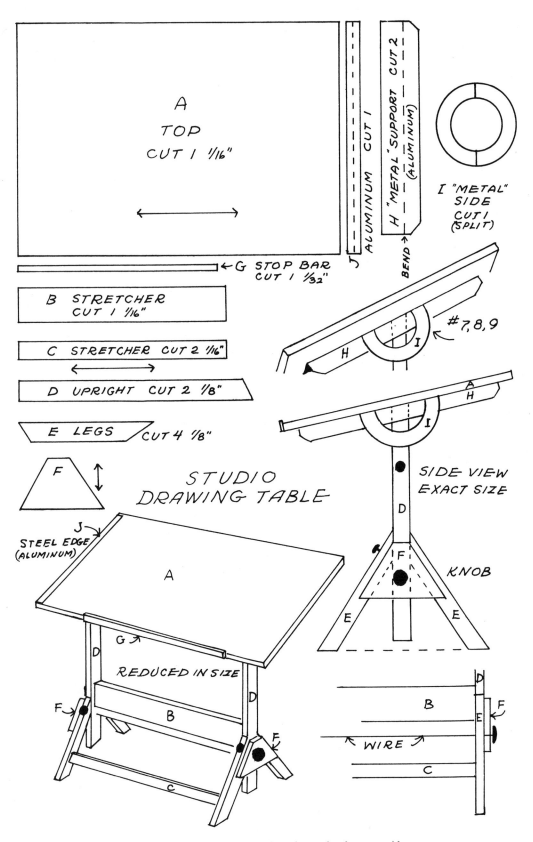

A
TOP
CUT 1 1/16"

ALUMINUM CUT 1

H "METAL" SUPPORT CUT 2
(ALUMINUM)

I "METAL" SIDE CUT 1
(SPLIT)

← G STOP BAR CUT 1 1/32"

J

BEND →

B STRETCHER CUT 1 1/16"

C STRETCHER CUT 2 1/16"

D UPRIGHT CUT 2 1/8"

E LEGS CUT 4 1/8"

F

STUDIO DRAWING TABLE

H

I

#7, 8, 9

A
H

I

SIDE VIEW EXACT SIZE

D

F

KNOB

E

E

J

STEEL EDGE (ALUMINUM)

A

G

REDUCED IN SIZE

D

D

F

B

F

c

D

B

F

E

WIRE

C

Fig. 6–6 Pattern and assemblage for studio drawing table.

ment. Lay flat on waxed paper. Dry well.

2. Glue side pieces (F) onto each leg structure.

3. Glue stretcher piece (B) between two leg structures.

4. Glue the two lower stretchers (C) between two front legs and two back legs.

5. Fold aluminum strip to 90-degree angle and glue to left side of table.

6. Center and glue stop bar (G) to front edge of table.

7. Glue legs (D) to metal supports (H).

8. Glue metal supports (H) to underside of table.

9. Glue metal sides (I) to (H) and (D).

10. Drill holes for insertion of screw knobs as indicated by bold dots in Fig. 6–6 and screw knobs into place.

11. The large knob at bottom right, is connected to a "rod" (copper wire) that runs across to the other side and is fastened with glue.

12. Finish with shellac or polyurethane.

How to Make a Tabouret

Pattern and assembly guide for the tabouret are provided in Fig. 6–7.

MATERIALS

Sheets of pine, $1/16''$ and $1/8''$; jumplinks for drawer pull.

DIRECTIONS

1. Glue sides (A) to back piece (B).

2. Glue bottom piece (C) into place.

3. Glue top piece (C) into place. Set it down $1/16''$ from top, creating a backstop area.

4. Glue middle section (C) into place, allowing $1/2''$ space for drawer.

5. Construct drawer, checking for fit; sand where necessary.

6. Add link drawer pull.

7. Center and glue base piece (D) onto bottom.

8. Using fine sandpaper, round the edges of the top counter and outside edges of front. Shellac.

How to Make an Open-Back Painted Chair

Pattern parts and assembly guide are provided in Fig. 6–8.

MATERIALS

Pine wood, $1/16''$ and $1/8''$; $1/8''$ wooden dowel; round toothpicks; acrylic paint for design.

DIRECTIONS

1. Sand seat of chair to acquire a little curvature and shape. See side view of seat in Fig. 6–8.

2. Using chisel-edge cutter and needle files, create small turnings on dowel legs as shown in Fig. 6–8. Taper bottom of each leg.

3. On underside of chair seat (A), rout out a small area where each chair leg will be glued.

4. Glue two front legs (D) into position. Notice the angle. Allow to dry thoroughly.

5. Glue front stretcher (E) into position, just less than halfway up from bottom.

6. Glue two back legs (D) into position. Allow to dry thoroughly.

7. Glue back stretcher (F) and side stretchers (G) into position. These must fit snugly, so it may be necessary to make new cuttings.

8. Sand edges of front outside curved areas of back (B).

9. Glue back (B) and splat (C) into position, tilting backward slightly. Dry thoroughly.

10. Paint entire chair a reddish-brown color.

11. Using gold paint and an artist's brush #000, stripe the turning on front

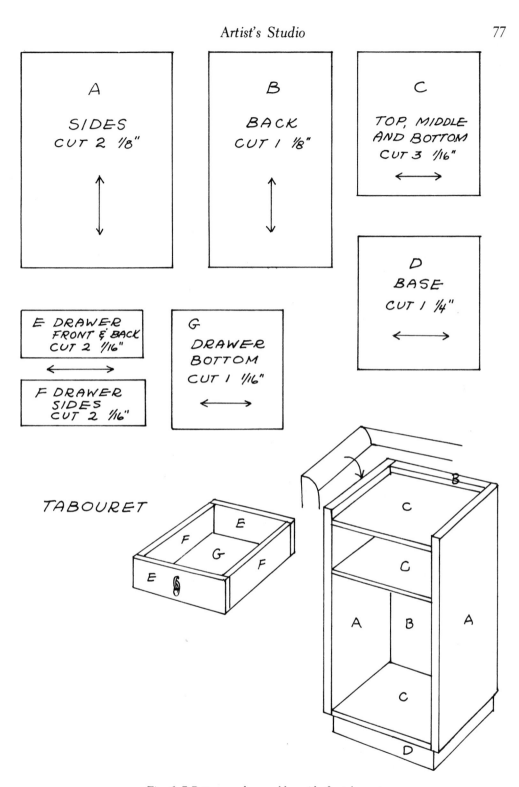

Fig. 6–7 Pattern and assembly guide for tabouret.

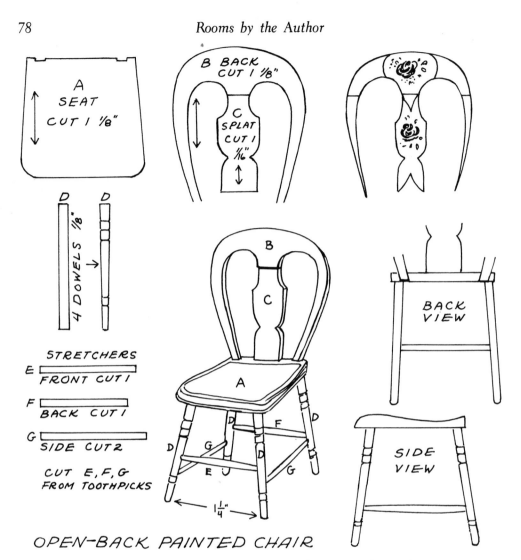

OPEN-BACK PAINTED CHAIR

Fig. 6–8 Pattern for open-back painted chair, made from pine and painted dark brown.

legs; paint stripes on chair seat and side and front areas of seat; also follow design pattern for back (B) and splat (C). Paint floral design on (B) and (C) with red flowers and green leaves.

How to Make a Worktable

Fig. 6–9 provides the pattern and assembly guide for the table.

MATERIALS

Pine wood, $1/16''$ and $1/8''$.

DIRECTIONS

1. Glue large sidepieces (B) and small sidepieces (C) to underside of table. There will be a small recess all around.

2. Glue four legs (D) up into each corner.

3. Glue supports (E) into position.

4. Glue cross bar (F) into position.

5. Shellac.

6. Add some smudges of paint to different parts of table. After all, it *is* a worktable.

How to Make Art Supplies

A wide variety of artist's supplies and studio accessories is shown in Fig. 6–10.

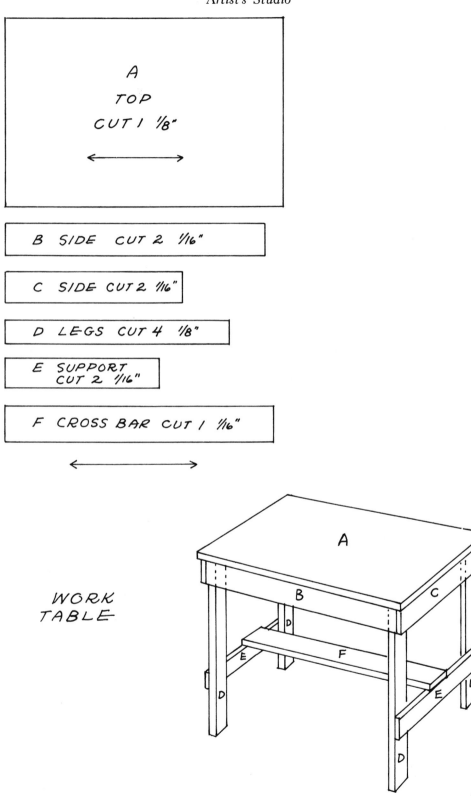

Fig. 6–9 Pattern for worktable, made from pine.

Palette

Cut palette shape out of balsa, pine or basswood, using pattern in Fig. 6–10. Sand, lacquer, then add dabs of color; smear some around on surface. Add double tin palette cups to edge. These are two primers from fired cartridges (*be sure they have been fired*). They can also be made out of a cut drinking straw and painted silver.

Brushes

Artist's brushes are toothpick handles, painted black. Wider brushes are handles shaped out of $1/32''$-thick wood.

1. Hold cluster of hair in fingers and cut off top of hair, straight.
2. Saturate top of cut hair with thick white glue. Push handle against glue. Dry several hours. With scissors, trim hair as shown in Fig. 6–10.
3. Paint silver or aluminum color partially down over hair and also above onto handle. Color rest of handle black, white, yellow or whatever. Human hair or fine hair from discarded brushes can be used.

Tubes, Jars of Paint, Ink Bottle

Tubes, jars and bottles are created from various small dowels. Indentations are incised on "jars" for lids, which are then painted white. Rest of jar is "paint" colored. Tubes are chisel-shaped at bottom. The cap is a straight pin with round head. Half the head is cut with chisel-edge cutter and glue is inserted into top of dowel "tube." Paint silver color, then color a band on top of each of red, green, blue, etc.

Sandpad

Shape a piece of $1/32''$ wood. Add two pieces of very fine sandpaper to top.

Pencil Sharpener

Shape a piece of wood and set on small base. Glue thin slice of dowel to left side. Handle is twisted paper clip. Add seed bead knob and paint silver.

Spatulas

Shape handles out of toothpicks and cut blades out of metal pouring spout from boxes of salt, cereal, dishwashing detergent.

Brayer

Cut a piece of $1/8''$ dowel. Paint black. Attach to a handle shaped from a black hairpin.

Metal Bowls

The prongs are removed from furniture glides, which come in different sizes.

Stretched Canvas

Construct stretchers out of small strips of wood. Cover with lightweight buckram "canvas."

Pastel Set

Construct box out of card. Pastels are assorted colored pencils with wooden outer covering removed.

Pencils and Pen Holder

There are different thicknesses of bristle on corn broom. Select straight pieces and cut to size needed, a mite over $1/2''$ length. Color pencils yellow, bottom tan and tiny black tip for lead. Paint pen holders black. Cut actual pieces of eraser to make erasers.

Art Book

Use layers of paper, starting with a note pad. Cut through layers, keeping glued edge for binding side. Glue thin

Fig. 1 Within a shallow sectional box, a family group is personalized in miniature, thus becoming an "heirloom."

Fig. 2 A cheese box becomes a delightful miniature room for a little girl. It can be folded up to "travel" with its owner.

Fig. 3 Red flocked wall covering, pillars and planters help create a dignified Banquet Room.

Fig. 4 Although food can be presented in many ways, it's hard to surpass an appetizing smorgasbord and dessert table. What calories!

Fig. 5 Painted and decorated "pottery" of many shapes and sizes, all made from papier mâché egg cartons, are properly placed in a pottery showroom which is also made from egg cartons and a corrugated box.

Fig. 6 Using contrasting textures, a white and gold bedroom becomes a plush, elegant fantasy room.

Fig. 7 The Needlework Shop is furnished with all the products necessary for a well-run business.

Fig. 8 Duplicating the furniture and accessories of the famous *Belle* of *Amherst* production, a miniature set comes alive.

Fig. 9 A French armchair, small Victorian sofa, writing desk and chair, and parquet box are a few of The Belle of Amherst set miniature furnishings.

Fig. 10 Miniature seashells individually plucked from Florida sand end up as whimsical animals, wall plaques, specimen shells and more in an orderly Seashell Shop.

Fig. 11 Tiny seashell wall arrangements can be developed and created in a variety of ways. Different backgrounds and frames add greater interest.

Fig. 12 An entrance hall (at left) and a Victorian living room combine to make an interesting miniature arrangement.

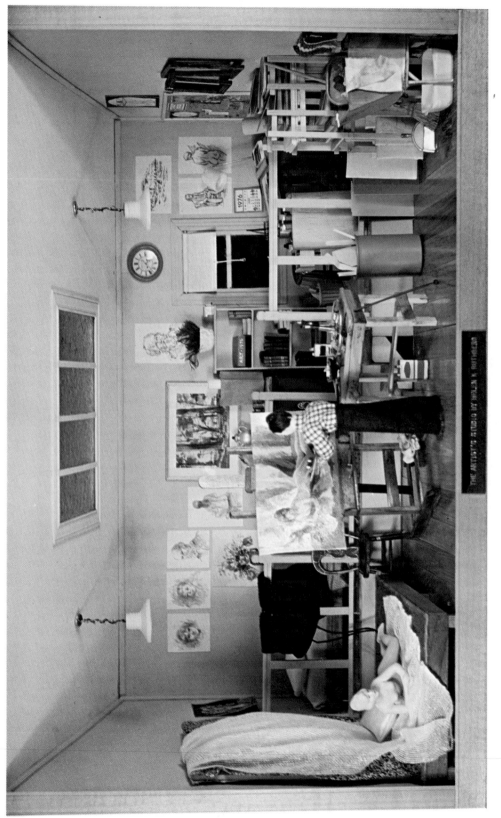

Fig. 13 The Artist's Studio is completed with special equipment and art supplies, all essential to the working artist.

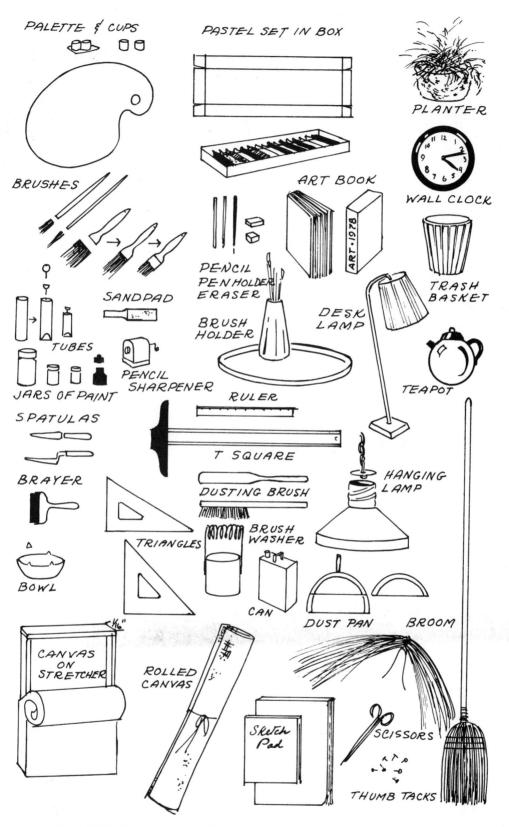

PALETTE & CUPS

PASTEL SET IN BOX

PLANTER

BRUSHES

ART BOOK

ART · 1978

WALL CLOCK

PENCIL
PEN HOLDER
ERASER

SANDPAD

TRASH
BASKET

BRUSH
HOLDER

DESK
LAMP

TUBES

PENCIL
SHARPENER

JARS OF PAINT

TEAPOT

SPATULAS

RULER

T SQUARE

BRAYER

HANGING
LAMP

DUSTING BRUSH

TRIANGLES

BRUSH
WASHER

BOWL

CAN

DUST PAN

BROOM

CANVAS
ON
STRETCHER

ROLLED
CANVAS

Sketch
Pad

SCISSORS

THUMB TACKS

Fig. 6–10 Guide to instructions for all manner of studio supplies and accessories.

leather or imitation leather to fit around "pages" of book. On binding add the lettering, ART–1978, or year of your choice. This is a good way to date the contemporary set and the year it was made.

Brush Holder on Tray

Cut bottom part off used Lucite Bic pen. Use heated knife to cut through plastic. Tray is discarded lid from cocoa box or end of a small frozen juice container.

Ruler

Glue a piece of aluminum foil between two very thin slivers of wood or, for steel ruler, use metal pouring spout. Apply delicate black markings along edge.

T Square

The T part is cut out of a plastic insert used to stiffen collars of men's shirts. Paint black. The long section is a very thin strip of wood (veneer or imitation wood glued on top of $1/32''$ strip of acrylic. There are also steel T Squares.

Dusting Brush

Cut the handle shape out of hardwood. Add bristles as described for paintbrushes.

Triangles

Cut shapes of triangles out of $1/32''$ acrylic or clear acetate.

Cans for Turpentine or Thinner

Cut basic shape from block of wood. Size will vary, depending upon your need. Paint silver. Paint on an identifying label or, with luck, glue on a small label from a catalogue. Shape handle from links or whatever and cut pouring

spout from smallest dowel. Paint silver and glue in place.

Brush Washer

Container is small metal lid. Handle is a spring from used cartridge pen, shaped and glued to side.

Rolls of Canvas

Use anything that might resemble canvas material rolled up and tied . . . lightweight buckram, wide adhesive tape, fine fabrics stiffened with diluted white glue.

Planter

Cut a protruding portion out of a papier mâché egg carton. Paint with acrylic and glue mixture. Plant an air fern.

Wall Clock

Cut face of clock from a catalogue and fit within plastic cafe-curtain ring.

Small Trash Basket

Cover a thimble with very small pieces of wood all around the outside.

Lamp

Attach toothpaste-tube top "shade" to twisted paper clip (large size) and attach to a base. This is then glued to top of drawing table.

Teapot

Attach small button and seed bead as cover to top of wooden bead. Add dowel spout and link handle. Paint silver.

Hanging Lamp

Cut off upper part of toothpaste tube to attain shape (Fig. 6–10). Catch chain through gold sequin and glue sequin to opening of tube.

Dust Pan

Save two lift-off covers from cheese containers. Cut one lid as shown in Fig. 6–10. Glue onto second lid. Add tip from ballpoint pen for handle.

Broom

Cut several 3″ strands of bristles from cobweb broom. These are thin and flexible. Catch tightly together at top with bead wire. Pull down tightly, concealing wire. Saturate top area with *thick* white glue. Force antiseptic stick down through top (or drill small hole *after* drying process). Wind masking tape around bottom of bristles and allow to dry thoroughly. Glue and wind silver wire about handle, close to bristles. Remove tape. Apply more glue and wind red-colored thread around thrice at top. Cut bottom of bristles straight.

Towel Bar

Select two simple bead caps and attach a shaped large wire paper clip to each one. Glue well, using a little cotton within caps to secure.

CHAPTER
7

Banquet Room

When we relate to food, our four senses of sight, smell, touch and taste are very much involved and, if you want to go out on a limb and include a hissing, crackling fire that is char-broiling a steak, you might even include hearing.

In miniature, the finished food involves only "sight" and, once you elicit exclamations of awe from admirers of your culinary skill, then you know you've passed the test for miniature gourmet cook.

An attractive restaurant and a desire to create a smorgasbord and dessert table culminated in The Banquet Room (Fig. 7–1 and color section, Figs. 3 and 4).

How to Finish Interior Walls and Floor

This is a standard basic box, devoid of windows or other extra features. Interest is provided by the architectural elements of pilasters and built-in planters and columns, not to mention the food!

Upholstery carpeting is glued down first. The upper part of the room is covered with red flock paper (Contact) and the wainscoting is a veneer from Constantine's. A chair rail from Northeast-

ern is added. The upright wall pilasters are strips of pine, $^1/_8''$ thick by $^3/_4''$ wide. Miniature trim molding with a fluted design (Northeastern #DCC-16) is glued on top. Extra, thicker blocks of pine are measured for top and bottom (Fig. 7–5). All are fitted, stained, then glued into place (Figs. 7–2 and 7–3). Carved molding, purchased at a home care center, is fitted, cut, stained and glued at top of wall for cove molding.

Panel frames are made from miniature $^5/_{64}''$ cove molding and glued onto flock background. The center area has a "greeting card" mural within the panel.

Wall fixtures are made from metal button tops, filigree bead caps, deodorant roll-on balls and copper tubing that is twisted and shaped.

Two tables are simply made of pine and stained. Covered with cotton damask material, each table is ready to receive delicious food.

Top of box is glued and nailed into place.

Box planters and pillars of $^3/_4''$ dowel, previously planned for, are built, fitted, stained and glued into place (see Fig. 7–5). Two very small plastic nose-spray bottles are cut to fit within planters as a

Fig. 7–1 The striking background of the Banquet Room features red velour Contact paper and a wainscoting of special wood veneer. Light fixtures are made from button shanks, bead caps, copper tubing and roll-on deodorant balls and centered on panels. All woodwork except wainscoting is stained a deep mahogany. Lastly, the damask-covered tables are resplendent with luscious food.

Fig. 7–2 A think-ahead plan is important when building special wall units using pilasters, wainscoting and panels. Basic tables are constructed of pine and stained dark.

Fig. 7–3 With everything glued into place, the most sensible way to hold everything down until dry is to use a good-quality masking tape.

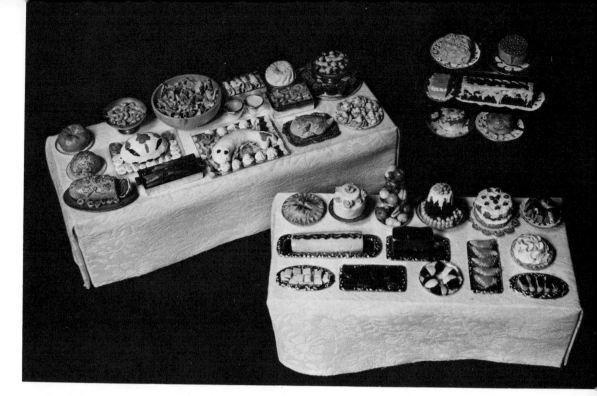

Fig. 7–4 Two tables and a purchased baker's rack, laden with food, will whet anyone's appetite. Directions for all foods are supplied in this chapter.

waterproof lining. Real plants (sedum) are planted within bottles.

Extra features are large corner urns made from finials, turned upside-down. Cut-down paper cups, painted gold, are added to top and hold air fern.

A baker's rack is placed behind the dessert table and also holds a fine sampling of sweets (Fig. 7–4). Yes, the rack is my one purchase for this room, an allowable luxury. I say luxury because look at the time it saved me and *time* is one thing I can't buy.

The food, made from plastic modeling compound, is colorfully displayed and looks delicious enough to whet anyone's appetite.

How to Make Pilasters and Banquet Tables

Pilasters are flat columns or half-round columns placed against walls or other architectural structures, such as mantels. Pattern and assembly guide are provided in Fig. 7–5.

Pilasters

MATERIALS

Pine or other woodstrips, $1/8''$ x $3/4''$ and $1/4''$ x $3/4''$; Northeastern Scale Model molding DCC-16.

DIRECTIONS

1. Cut two blocks of wood (B), $1/4''$ deep, $3/4''$ wide and $5/8''$ high.

2. Measure strip of wood (A) to fit within the two blocks to fill height of room. Strip is $3/4''$ wide and $1/8''$ deep.

3. Fit and glue on top of strip (A) a piece of DCC-16 fluted wood (C).

4. Stain or paint as you choose and glue all units into position on wall.

Smorgasbord Tables

Pattern parts for the table are supplied in Fig. 7–5.

MATERIALS

Pine, $1/8''$ and $1/4''$.

87

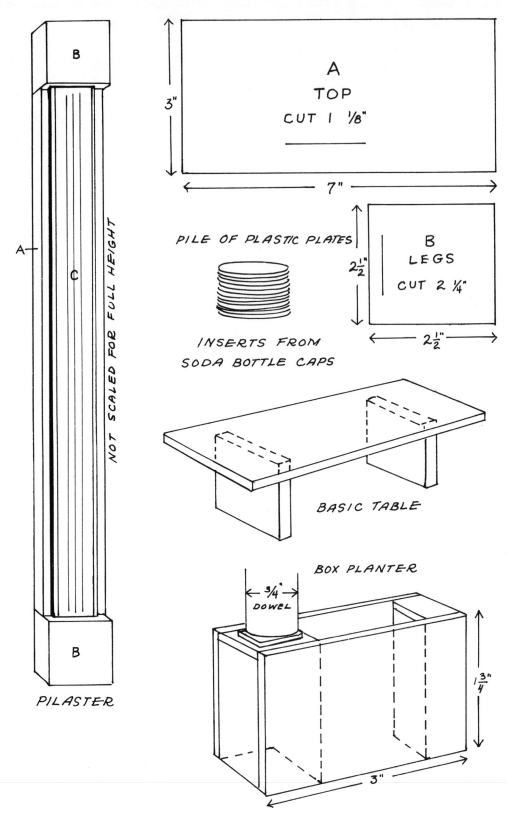

B

A
TOP
CUT 1   ⅛"

3"

7"

PILE OF PLASTIC PLATES

B
LEGS
CUT 2 ¼"

2½"

2½"

INSERTS FROM
SODA BOTTLE CAPS

A

C

B

NOT SCALED FOR FULL HEIGHT

PILASTER

BASIC TABLE

BOX PLANTER

¾"
DOWEL

1 ¾"

3"

Fig. 7–5 Patterns and assembly guide for pilasters, basic table and box planters.

DIRECTIONS

1. Sand and stain all cutout pieces.
2. Glue legs (B) to top (A) as shown in drawing.
3. Cover with a tablecloth that folds under at corners and extends to floor. Cotton damask is recommended.

How to Make Food
For the Feast

Patterns and sketches for a wide assortment of foods are provided in Fig. 7–6.

MATERIALS

Bread dough or a plastic modeling compound, such as Sculpey or Pendo; acrylic paints; small artist's brushes #000; lacquer spray; *and* any kind of implement that helps shape the food, such as a paring knife, used Bic ballpoint pen and protective cover, hatpin, toothpicks, stylus, small art brush handle.

DIRECTIONS

Modeling food is mostly manipulating with your fingers and making use of a few ordinary implements. Noting the proper size of food and discerning appropriate colors are equally important, since these two accuracies help make your food believable.

Sometimes it's necessary to push, pull, punch, stretch, roll, cut, flatten and squeeze to attain a reasonable semblance of the real product. Shaping is often a matter of trial and error . . . but oh, how thrilling it is to accidentally discover a new way to render a food product.

Many times, two shades of one color will make a product look more authentic. For instance, two shades of green on the asparagus or lettuce, two shades of color on baked products.

Crusts on pies and breads are best painted with an ochre color, lightened with white and sometimes deepened with brown or sepia for browned effects. I call this "crust" color and refer to it as such in the text.

For some foods you will find a suitable substitute shape using a piece of cut dowel. Large dowels become the bases for cheeses, short cakes, frosted cakes and layer cakes. Smaller dowels can be made into bologna and salami and sliced dowels can even become sliced fruit (oranges, lemons, tomatoes), cookies and meat.

Likewise, small blocks of wood are transformed into square cakes, frosted cakes and seven-layer cakes. There are square molds, rectangular cheeses and very small dessert bars.

Personally, I usually prefer to model the product. There's something too rigid in appearance with dowel-made food.

Sauces are many. These are dessert sauces (fudge, strawberry, butterscotch), cream sauces (white, cheese), sour cream sauces, meat sauces, salad dressings, and glazes. When necessary, these are made with the appropriate color paint with a little white glue added to the mixture. Dribbled onto some food, it provides the finished look.

Stuffed products, such as green peppers, orange cups and mushrooms, get their start as "balls," punched in with an implement. But perhaps it's better to just describe the food shown in Fig. 7–6 and how it's attained. However, remember that *all food is hardened before any color is applied.*

Hot and Cold Food

Molds are initially modeled by hand. If it's a ring mold, an implement of appropriate size is pushed down through the center. An impression on a *gelatin* mold is made with the tip of a paring knife, regularly and gently pushed against the sides. A flat top is cut off with the same sharp knife. A *cheese mold* with parsley covering is dipped into dark-green painted celery flakes.

A *fish mold* is shaped and black seed bead eyes (black olives) are glued in head. Fish is hardened. Paint with a light yellow glaze. Thick lines of white paint are added for eyebrows, mouth, back and tail decoration, which is filled in with orange paint.

Beef Wellington is modeled and one end is sliced off. Small squiggly designs are shaped as shown in Fig. 7–6 and pressed onto surface. Harden. Outside is painted crust color, with dabs of darker color in and around crust ornamentation. Inside is painted with three colors: outer part of crust (ochre) shows; next a thin dark green (parsley); lastly, rust red color for meat. With brush tip, add some small marking of fat and grain.

Stuffed mushrooms, chicken croquettes in pastry shell and *stuffed peppers* all start with balls, appropriately sized. The pastry shell is flattened. All receive a different-size implement pushed into the center. Mushrooms and peppers are shaped and thinned out around implement. Flute outside of peppers. Harden. Stuff mushrooms with crushed thyme and glue. Stuff peppers with celery flakes and glue. Color mushrooms tan outside, brown inside. Color peppers dark green outside, dark brown inside. Pastry shell design is shaped with knife tip. Small cone-shaped piece is placed in center. Harden. Pastry is "crust" colored; when dry, cream sauce/ glue mixture is painted over center and dripped around pastry.

Asparagus spears are shaped with different thicknesses. The end is teased out with the tip of a hatpin. It will look

mutilated and that's fine. Harden. Apply medium green color; later, add slightly darker color toward other end, including tip.

Belgian carrots are shaped by hand. Harden and paint "carrot" color.

Shrimp are shaped by hand. Harden. Paint light orange and later add a spotted coloring of tan and orange.

Lettuce and tomato salad: lettuce is an extremely thin piece of modeling compound, bent, twisted, curled. Harden. Paint a couple shades of green. Tomato is a modeled semiround, cut into quarters. Harden. Paint outside bright red-orange, inside orange. Add tiny seed markings with brush, if possible.

Deviled eggs are modeled into egg shape, then sliced in half. Harden, Paint egg white. In center, add thick yellow glue mixture, piling it up a little. Be careful not to go near edge. Leave white margin showing.

Lemon slices are tiny balls pushed down flat with finger. Cut in two with knife. Harden. Outside ridge (skin) is painted dark yellow. Inside is lighter yellow. Add tiny fine radiating lines of white.

Tomato garnish: roll out a long, thin piece of clay. Flatten thin. Roll back up, forming a rose. This is like cutting the skin from a real tomato. Harden. Color red-orange tomato color.

Desserts

Piecrusts are clay pushed into a screw-on soda bottle top that has been cut down in depth to $1/16''$. The clay is piled up higher in center and very high for a *meringue-topped pie* (see Fig. 7–6). Create impressions for crimped edging and include slashed steam openings. Swirl "meringue" around until satisfied, but remember to leave a crust

HOT & COLD FOOD
MOLDS

CHEESE   CREPE   POTATO SALAD   FISH MOLD ~ LEMON

MUSHROOMS   DEVILED EGGS   BEEF WELLINGTON

CROQUETTE

MEATBALLS   STUFFED PEPPER   TOMATO GARNISH   TURKEY   (CHICKEN) SMALLER   TOMATO

ASPARAGUS   CARROTS   SHRIMP   LETTUCE

DESSERTS

FRUIT PIE   LAYER CAKE   SEVEN LAYER CAKE   LEMON MERINGUE PIE

PLUM PUDDING   BUNDT CAKE   JELLY ROLL

SQUARES

STRAWBERRY SHORT CAKE   CHERRY CHEESE CAKE   APPLE TURNOVERS   FRUIT   MOCHA FROSTED CAKE

Fig. 7–6 Modeling foods for the Banquet Room (see Fig. 7–4).

91

edge showing. Harden. Paint crust color; add darker brown color on raised portions. Add red coloring for *cherry pie* steam openings and a little juice running down crust. Paint meringue white. Add ochre-brown color on crests and peaks with finger tip.

Cakes of all shapes and sizes are modeled by hand (or dowel may be used). Harden. *Layer cake* has pink icing, decorated with raspberry-colored roses and buds, made like tomato rose. *Seven-layer cake* is deep chocolate outside. Add painted cream and chocolate-colored layers inside. *Bundt cake* is shaped and hole punched. A slice is cut out. It is crust colored and topped with chocolate sauce mixture of paint and glue.

Jelly roll is shaped. Paint pink outside and white on both ends, topped with swirl pattern of deep raspberry color. Raspberry "swiggles" are added to top. *Plum pudding* is shaped. Harden. Paint dark brown. Add thick white paint/glue mixture for sauce topping. Glue tiny grapes, previously hardened and painted light green, on top of sauce and around base of pudding, which has been glued to a platter.

Strawberry short cake: prepare two 1/8″ layers of cake (paint crust color) and several shaped strawberries (paint luscious red). Prepare very thick white paint/glue mixture for whipped cream. Add to top of bottom layer. Place several strawberries on top. Be sure color of red doesn't come off onto white. If so, wait, then proceed. Glue on top crust. Add whipped cream to top, dribbling some down the side. Space and arrange other strawberries on top.

Cherry cheese cake is shaped 1/4″ high. Paint crust color. Very tiny, hardened cherry shapes are glued on top. Cherries are coated with bright red paint/glue mixture and dribbled down sides.

Apple turnovers are a thin, round, flat piece of clay. Fold over. Cut excess away for triangular shape. Using hatpin, crimp two edges. Paint crust color. *Brownies* are cut and painted dark brown and *strawberry squares* are painted light pink. A square-shaped *mocha frosted cake* is probably the easiest of all. Cover with thick swirls of tan-colored paint/glue mixture. Want to add crushed nuts? Sprinkle sawdust onto gluey surface. This won't do much for a mocha cake, but it will enhance a chocolate one.

CHAPTER
8

Seashell Shop

After spending endless hours plucking itsy-bitsy seashells out of a pile of "crushed sand," it was imperative to show off these miniature beauties . . . and what better way than to create a Seashell Shop (see color Figs. 10 and 11)! Observing a few of the real shops proved that some were orderly and others were inclined to be messy. Orderliness is more acceptable to my Virgo nature, so seashells are neatly lined up for display or patterned into little creatures resembling mice, ducks, owls, pelicans and other birds. Additional whimsical, handmade novelties are 3/4″ seashell dolls, cylindrical trees, jewelry, flowers and mushrooms. Several assorted wall groupings, specially designed within attractive frames, are neatly arranged on the wall (Fig. 8–1).

How to Finish the Interior

With the exceptions of the Carlson showcase and sculptured pelican, all furnishings are made from scratch or from found materials.

The walls of the shop are covered with fine-quality artist's painting canvas and the carpeting is upholstery material.

The left portion of the shop is partitioned off. A plastic container originally used to hold primers (used for gun loading) is painted and held up between dowels. Holes were drilled through both and small pins inserted through plastic sides into dowel to make a divider used to show off specimen shells (Fig. 8–2). Behind this are bowls of shells and other arrangements.

The right side of the shop shows more seashell artistic endeavor and provides a small area in back of showcase for transacting business (Fig. 8–3).

How to Make a Floor Display Unit

The display unit shown in Fig. 8–4 can be made following pattern in Fig. 8–5.

MATERIALS

Sheets of pine wood, 1/16″ and 1/8″; cove molding, 3/32″.

DIRECTIONS

1. Distress the wood with cuts and gouges.
2. Stain all pieces of wood dark.
3. Starting with bottom shelf (D), glue to each side piece (E) as indicated by dotted lines on drawing.

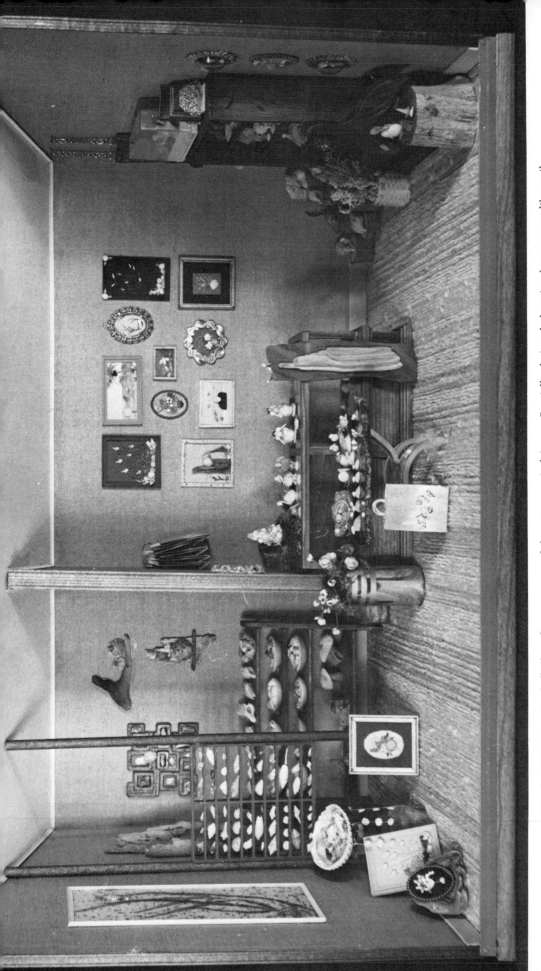

Fig. 8–1 Miniature Seashell Shop features many of the attractions that visitors delight in seeing in a real shop. Shells are displayed as specimens, arrangements, critters and other whimsical items. Specially designed shopping bags are readily available. Many seashells are as small as $1/16''$ in size.

Fig. 8–2 Left side of shop features specimen shells and bowls of shells ready for the customer to select. The divider makes a nice display unit. The large mural was cut from a greeting card and framed. Seashell flowers rest within cosmetic bottle top. Other arrangements and scallop owls on back wall fill out the area.

4. Continue with each successive shelf.

5. Cut cove molding to fit under each shelf on both sides. Glue against undershelf and against side (E) for extra shelf support.

How to Make a Wall Display Unit

Fig. 8–6 supplies pattern parts for the display case shown in Fig. 8–3.

MATERIALS

Sheets of pine wood, $^1/_{16}''$ and $^1\!/_8''$; $^1\!/_2''$ pine for base; mirror.

DIRECTIONS

1. Distress the wood with cuts and gouges.

2. Bevel top areas on front and sides of base piece (D), as shown in Fig. 8–6.

3. Stain all pieces of wood dark.

4. Glue mirror (B) to left side of back piece (C). Allow to dry thoroughly.

5. Glue sides (A) to base piece (D).

6. Add extra support to back of mirror and wood where they are joined together. Glue a thin length of wood over both at seam line. Dry thoroughly.

7. Glue mirror and back (C) to sides (A).

Fig. 8–3 A specially constructed showcase holds an assortment of shell dishes, ashtrays, driftwood, arrangements and potted tulips, all ready for the customer. A fake aquarium display is made from a Dynamint dispenser and a large shell collage is mounted on wood. Specimen shells are set on logs and tiny oval shell floral arrangements are displayed under plastic domes. The pelican is a purchase.

8. Glue shelves (E) into position. Bottom shelf is 1¹/₂″ from base. Rest of shelves are spaced approximately 1″ apart. Avoid using glue near mirror.

9. Glue top (F) into place.

10. Glue supports (G) under each shelf at both ends.

How to Make Seashell Wall Arrangements

An endless array of fascinating arrangements can be devised, as shown in Figs. 8–7 and 8–8.

MATERIALS

Plenty of baby seashells, including cups, whelks, augers, cones, tusks, zebras, rice, boats, arks, scallops, lilacs; other bits of sea life, such as sea lace, sea fan, dried plant life; Northeastern miniature frame moldings; balsa wood strips; sandpaper.

DIRECTIONS

Although miniature arrangements are tiny, the variety can still be great. Directions will be pretty general, pointing out the small differences. Lettered steps refer to labels in Fig. 8–8.

96

Most frames are made from miniature molding. Others are balsa wood and the rest are jewelry findings or doodads.

A. Background and frame are painted one color (dark green or turquoise). Lacy material is sea fan with outer portion stripped off. Shells are grouped along bottom and whelks tip the tops. Dark area is crushed orange sea-lace fan.

B and C. Similar arrangements with blue, red or green velvet ribbon mats. Floral designs are glued onto lighter color of mat in a contrasting material.

D. Begin with a painted background of sky, sea and sand. The painted palm tree has three brown mustard-seed coconuts. Ducks on water and heron are made from seashells; shells are also sprinkled along bottom area.

E. These two are my favorites, with balsa-wood frames and sandpaper backgrounds. Balsa is painted same color as back and holes are punched in frame with compass point to simulate wormwood. Driftwood, dried sea life and seashell birds complete the group.

F. Frame and background are painted black. Dried purple sea life is tipped with baby ceriths. More shells are grouped along bottom.

Fig. 8–4 A free-standing display piece with graduating shelves is made of pine, distressed and stained a dark color. Along with specimen shells are "plastic egg carton" bowls, each holding a different variety of shells. Miniature mushroom coral is made into mushrooms.

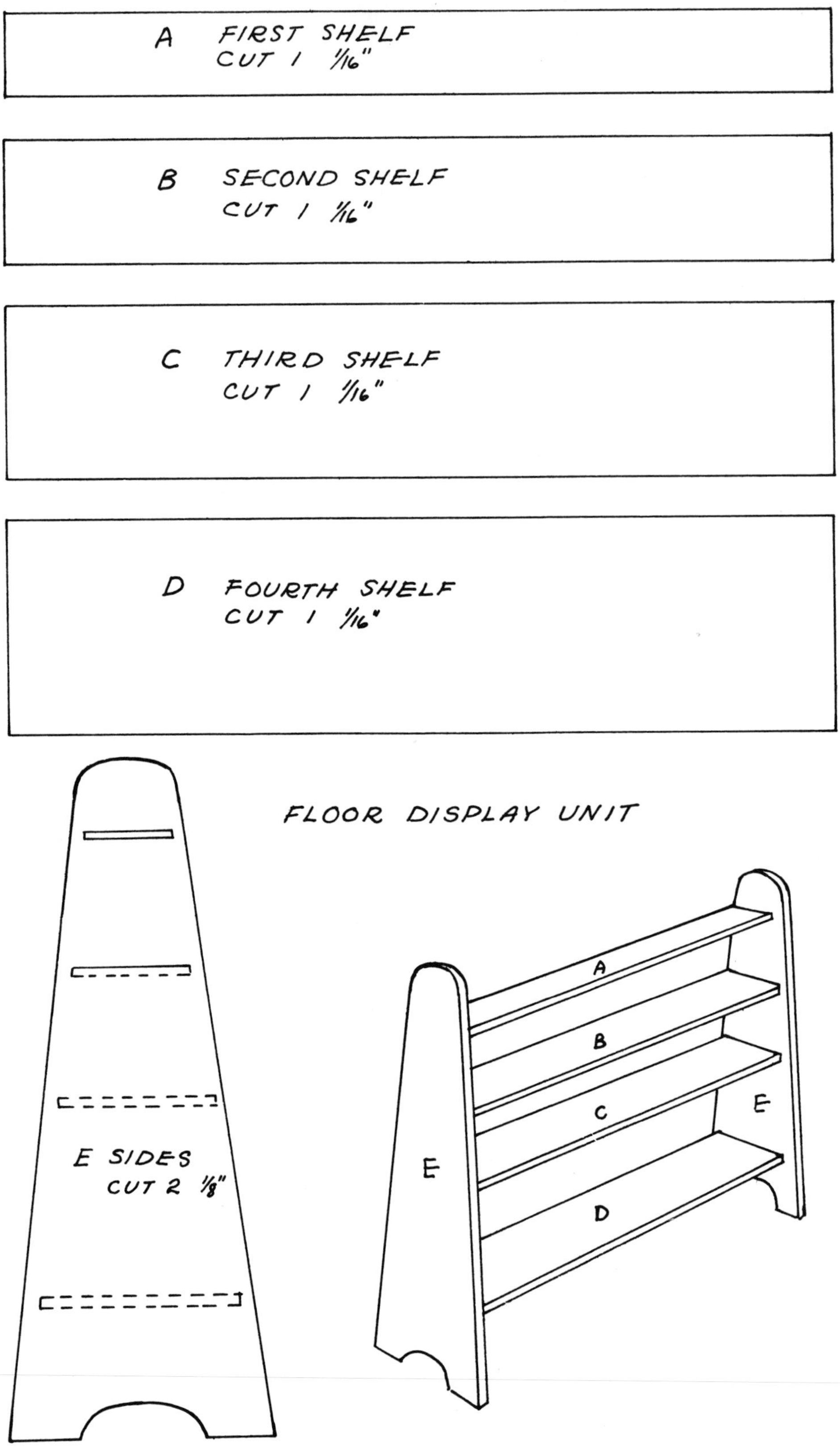
A FIRST SHELF
CUT 1 1/16"
B SECOND SHELF
CUT 1 1/16"
C THIRD SHELF
CUT 1 1/16"
D FOURTH SHELF
CUT 1 1/16"
FLOOR DISPLAY UNIT
E SIDES
CUT 2 1/8"
A
B
C
D
E
E

Fig. 8–5 Pattern parts and assembly guide for floor display unit.

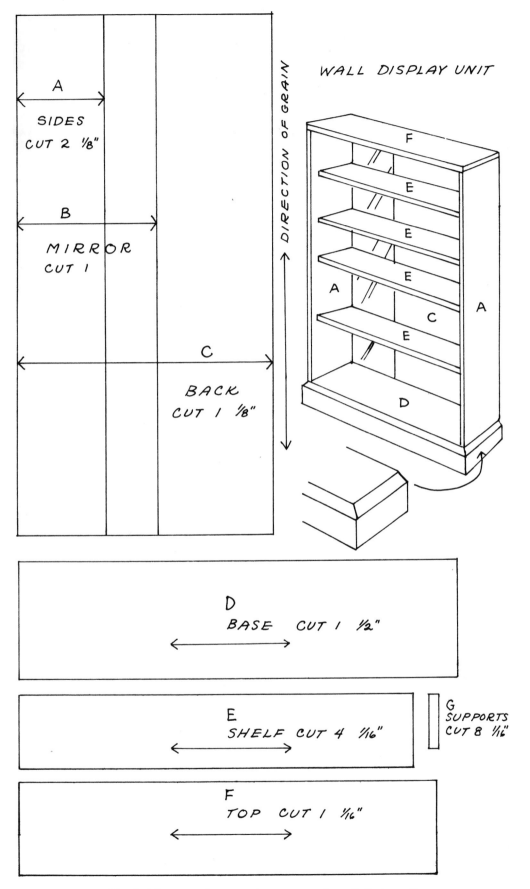

A

SIDES
CUT 2 ⅛"

B

MIRROR
CUT 1

C

BACK
CUT 1 ⅛"

DIRECTION OF GRAIN

WALL DISPLAY UNIT

F

E

E

A

E

C

A

E

D

D

BASE   CUT 1 ½"

E

SHELF CUT 4 ⁵/₁₆"

G
SUPPORTS
CUT 8 ⁵/₁₆"

F

TOP CUT 1 ⁵/₁₆"

Fig. 8–6 Pattern and construction sequence for wall display unit.

Fig. 8–7 Back wall of shop displays seashell arrangements within a grouping of frames, mostly handmade with a few from jewelry findings. Painted scenes, fabric and sandpaper are used behind the variety of arrangements. All designs are described in text.

G. Two versions of shell design on velvet paper background. The frames were devised from doodad findings.

H. Background is painted blue-green for water effect. Fish is rice shell with lilac shell fins and jingle shell tail. Frame is balsa wood.

I. Scallop shell becomes a basket for small shell flowers. The basket handle is gold bead wire. Jewelry finding frame.

J. Blue moiré background with green thread stems and baby ceriths atop piece of abalone.

K. The big one, a montage, is $1/8''$ wood which has been distressed. Singe the edges too, if desired. Twigs, driftwood and sea life are glued together in an attractive arrangement.

L. The proverbial shopping bag. Watercolor painted, the top area is blue, the bottom is green. Both colors fade into white where the seashell designs are inked in. String handles are attached.

M. A seashell mirror. Cut mirror to fit within frame molding and glue miniature shells around, keeping a pattern in the design.

N. Gift boxes are just thrown in to remind you that every shop should have some, plus note pads, pencil holder, and whatever else you care to add to the business scene.

How to Make Miniature Shell Novelties

Obviously, variety can exist in seashell miniatures. Figs. 8–9 and 8–10 show an assortment of critters and other interesting arrangements.

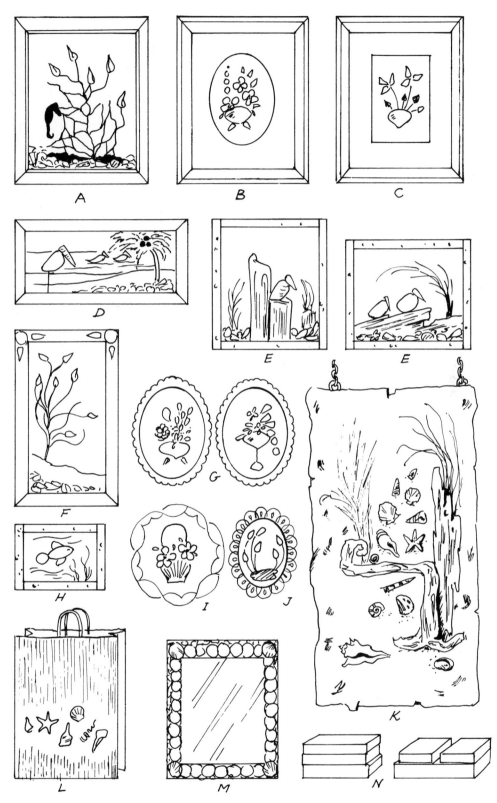

Fig. 8–8 A variety of wall arrangements and designs for shopping bag, shell mirror and montage.

Fig. 8–9 Tiny seashells become tiny replicas of duck and ducklings, assorted birds, mice, floral arrangements, dolls, candy dishes, sailboats and more. A beautiful piece of driftwood, resembling a mother and child, is mounted on thin wood. Small shells are packaged within 1/2" scallop shells and covered with cellophane wrapping.

Scallop shells make perfect *owls*, mounted on twigs, driftwood or other backgrounds. Add eyes and V-nose features with paint.

Mushrooms are made from very small mushroom shells glued onto thick twigs and then glued onto slab stone base.

Flowers are glued onto thin florist's wire. Tulips can be set within a pot made from quilling paper or several can be grouped together in a lipstick top or cosmetic bottletop. The baby whelk flowers are painted red.

Other little arrangements of baby whelks or baby ceriths are placed within a barnacle "vase" or conch shell.

The *mobile* is made of white baby cups glued to thread and attached to twig.

The *shell doll* takes a bit more patience. Start with piece of corn broom (A). Cotton will help in structuring.

Glue pair of cupshells near top (B). Starting at bottom (C), glue baby rose cups around for layered skirt. These will overlap. Glue small second layer around (D). Glue third layer of very small rose cups (E). Add a pair of white cup seashells for head (F). Glue on two small tusk shells for arms (G). Glue two lilac shells at top of each arm for sleeves (H). Paint black hair, dot eyes and dot read mouth. Add pink cupshell on back of head for bonnet (I).

Birds can be many and look different, depending upon your choice of shell combinations. *Swan* is ark shell body, baby whelk head and string neck, stiffened with glue. *Turkey* is two sizes of scallop shells, spaced and held together with glued cotton. Add baby whelk heard. *Parrot* is zebra shell head on marginella body. Beak is smallest whelk. Other birds are combinations of

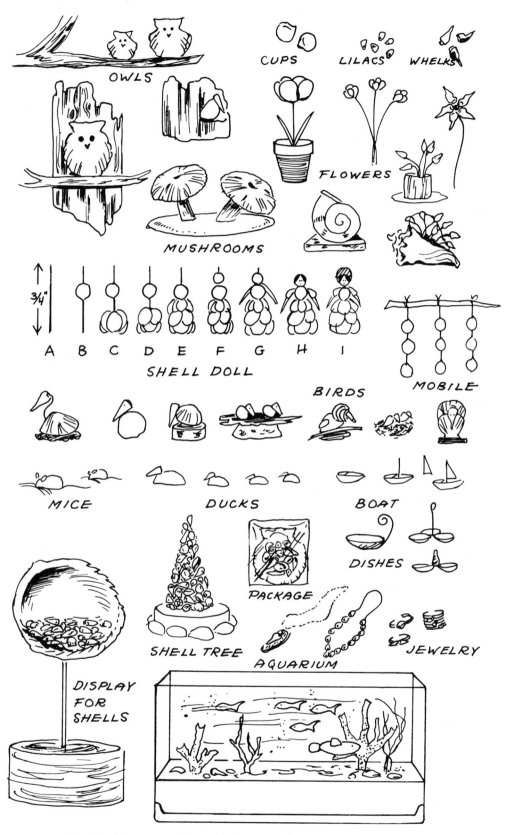

OWLS

CUPS   LILACS   WHELKS

FLOWERS

MUSHROOMS

3/4"

A B C D E F G H I

SHELL DOLL

MOBILE

BIRDS

MICE   DUCKS   BOAT

DISHES

PACKAGE

SHELL TREE   AQUARIUM   JEWELRY

DISPLAY FOR SHELLS

Fig. 8–10 Miniature replicas include critters, doll, aquarium and display stand.

103

different shell bodies and heads placed on bases of shell, cut twig, driftwood or a "nest" of cut thread.

Boat or slipper shells are made into *mice, ducks* and *sailboats,* of course. For *mouse,* add lilac ears, thread tail and hair whiskers. For *duck,* add small rice shell head. For *sailboat,* add tusk shell or toothpick for mast and small cutout sail of card.

Candy dishes have handles of wire, eyepin or whatever.

Package is several miniature shells resting in a scallop shell, all covered with cellophane.

Tree is shaped wood, covered with shells and mounted on a doodad base.

Display for shells: a long nail is hammered through a round of wood cut from a tree limb. A piece of driftwood is caught on top of nail and a 1½" rose

cockle is glued on top. A wide variety of miniature shells are carefully glued within cavity of cockle shell.

Jewelry can be made from lilac shells glued to thread for necklace. Filigree pendant features one specimen shell attached to jeweler's chain. Bracelets are links with added shells.

Aquarium display tank starts with an empty Dynamint container. Background is painted scene of fish, water, etc., on Bristol board. In foreground, base is filled with gluey cotton and bits of sea fan, coral and sea life are stuck into cotton. Sand is sprinkled on top while cotton is still moist. Make little fish, using rice shell bodies, lilac shell fins, jingle shell tails. Glue fish carefully onto sea fan or coral so they look suspended in water. Place background in rear and lower clear Lucite cover.

CHAPTER
9

Fantasy Bedroom

We have a long-haired cat and, like all cats, he selects the places where *he* wants to sleep. Since my bed is one of his favorite daily resting areas, the bedspread is a specially selected gray pattern which doesn't show soil. So what has this got to do with miniaturing? Nothing, except that I now have a small snowy-white bedroom minus the cat hairs. But, if I find a miniature snowy-white cat, you just *know* where he's going to end up.

Some of my earlier readers may recognize a few of these furnishings; yes, many were described in detail in *The Book of Miniatures*. Since it's wasteful to leave so many tiny things lying around in boxes, they made their way into this special white and gold room. When this room was exhibited, one male spectator was overheard exclaiming to his spouse, "Wouldn't you just *love* to fall into that?"

How to Decorate the Interior

This box room started with the frame first. The gold Victorian trim seemed to be appropriate for the idea that was yet to be fulfilled. So, the box was made to fit the size of the frame.

What followed is a plush white and gold bedroom, utterly feminine, with a mixture of Victorian and contemporary furnishings (Fig. 9–1 and color Fig. 6). The wall covering is silver, gold and white gift-wrap paper, topped with metallic braid trim. The headboard is a cornerpiece from a large Victorian frame mounted atop moiré covered, padded cardboard. The bedspread is the proverbial white lace-trimmed hankie with an added panel of lace down the front. The Victorian dressing table contrasts with the sleek line of the dresser, a kit from Realife Miniatures. Crystal chandelier, cherub egg holder (planter) and plush white acrylic carpeting complete the posh look.

Kits are marvelously useful in completing rooms and are available in wood, plastic and pewter. A wide variety of periods and styles is available from different companies that sell through dealers and stores.

For the bedroom, an easy-to-assemble dresser was selected but, instead of staining it as directed, I chose to paint it antique white, using special miniature paint merchandised by X-acto. Gold designs of loops and

Fig. 9-1 A posh white and gold Fantasy Bedroom is made even more ornate by contrasting textures of hard metal and soft, fluffy carpeting; by glitter of crystal chandelier and jeweled mirror; by trims of baroque designs and swirling curves. The cherub egg-holder "planter" at right contains real sedum plant.

Fig. 9–2 The dresser is made from an easy-to-assemble Realife Miniature kit. Halfway through, I parted company with the directions and painted the surface antique white, added gold designs and incorporated new drawer pulls.

spirals were painted onto drawers, sides, corners and base, thus continuing the prevailing gold and white motif (Fig. 9–2). The original drawer pulls were saved for something else and new modern pulls were made from small ¹/₈″ filigree rounds and white round heads of straight pins. Since I saw the perfect thing in a hardware store, it was easy to copy.

How to Create Dresser Designs

Dressers can be transformed into many different styles by adding designs appropriate to the decor. A few designs are offered in Fig. 9–3 to help the reader get started or to inspire some new thoughts about decorating furniture.

A. Curved linear designs are painted in gold on a solid-color background. Drawer pulls are white round heads of straight pins on top of small filigree bead caps, hammered flat.

B. Birds are stenciled or painted freehand onto wood background that has been stained or painted. Vine is added. Knobs are map pins.

C. A bold floral pattern is painted onto full front surface of chest. Map-pin knobs are staggered in position as they follow the "ribbon" design.

Fig. 9–3 Miniature furniture designs for stenciling or painting freehand.

WALL PLANTER

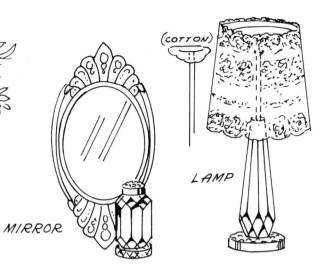

MIRROR

CRYSTAL JAR

(COTTON)

LAMP

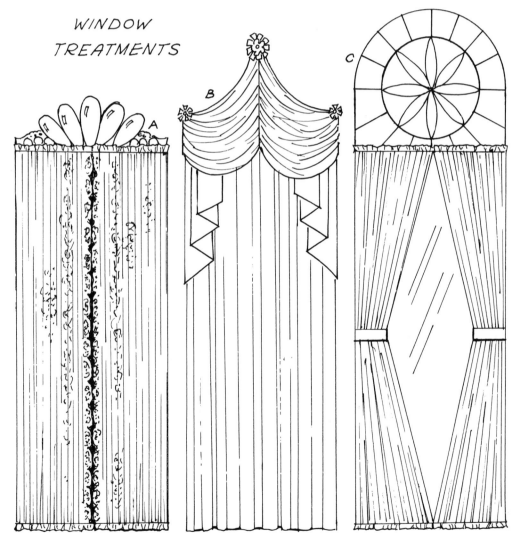

WINDOW
TREATMENTS

Fig. 9–4 Plans for bedroom accessories and window treatments.

109

D. Delicate bamboo design is painted onto solid-color background of lacquered red, black, white or yellow. Design is gold or a contrasting color.

E. Thin and thicker lines of color crisscross to form a plaid design on a solid color background. Drawer pulls are rice beads and copper wire.

How to Make Boudoir Accessories

Touches of elegance or luxury can be accomplished readily. It all depends upon your choice of materials and hardly anyone will dispute that "gold and glitter" do rank high. In addition to suggestions already mentioned, the drawings in Fig. 9–4 can offer further help.

Wall Planter

An elegant wall planter is made from a gold metal filigree napkin ring, cut in half. Open areas of bottom and side are fitted with colored or painted card that is glued into place. Dried, plastic or handmade plants and flowers are arranged within planter.

Mirror

Be watchful for antique brooches or pin findings that will accommodate a small mirror.

Crystal Jar

A large crystal bead is glued to a flat glass button and a gold metal doodad is added to top for cover.

Lamp

A large black crystal bead is glued to a gold button base. Shade is a jigger-size paper cup, painted yellow and covered with white lace. An antiseptic stick is glued and pushed down through bead opening. Gluey cotton is applied to top of stick and this is glued to inner center area of shade.

Window Treatments

A. Casement style drapery is achieved using shirred lace. The cut portion of a necklace is glued to the top for a special apex look.

B. This is a soft drape with jabot sides and an unusual swag top. Small round ornaments of your choice top it off.

C. For an unusual approach, create a stained-glass top, which is left uncovered. For privacy, the lower portion of the window uses casement style curtains, held back with ties.

CHAPTER
10

Needlework Shop

The Needlework Shop in Fig. 10–1 and color Fig. 7 was born out of a dormant hobby. Although my embroidery basket contained a few rejected projects, I knew that a miniature shop, once started, would never fade into that category of unfinished business. After visiting a few needlework departments and perusing the catalogues, the plans for a small shop rapidly fell into place.

How to Finish the Interior

The dimensions of this shop are 20″ wide, 12″ deep and 12″ high, the same as the demonstrated basic box room in Ch. 4.

A window is cut out of the back area before gluing box together (see Fig. 4–10). Platform of 5″ depth is glue/nailed into position, measuring for a three-step-up area with the steps that you are using, so plan accordingly. See the detailed instructions for planning and installing a platform in Ch. 6.

Printed wall covering is glued to back and two side areas as far as platform ends (Fig. 10–3). This is a pretty floral print cloth. For pasting, I use a white glue diluted with water and brush this onto the wood surface. Then I wet the material, which has already been cut to size and place it into position. The wetness allows easy maneuvering. With brayer, press the moisture and bubbles out of the material for smooth fit. Allow to dry thoroughly.

Next, lay down floor covering of your choice. I used vinyl floor tile that resembles a slate pattern. This is adhered to the wood base with epoxy cement.

Measure, cut and glue molding around window area after glass has been fastened in place.

Mix a color that goes well with the wall covering and place in empty deodorant jar, with lid. Make enough for later touch-up use. Paint window molding.

Place masking tape along floor segment against front wall areas and proceed to paint uncovered left and right walls.

Measure, construct and lay in steps (Fig. 10–4). On left, add a railing. Stain railing and paint posts (see Fig. 10–2).

Construct shelf area as shown in Fig. 10–4 and paint with color mixture. Then add carved trim.

Fig. 10–1 "Needlework from the Heart" is the name given to this shop. Everything is either made from scratch or from contrived materials. A pattern background is established with fabric wall covering and vinyl "slate" flooring. Wood furnishings are finished in dark stain to contrast with the rose paint on walls, door, shelving and trim. Accessories are placed in and on proper, useful structures. The name of the shop is painted on the outside of the window and the same design becomes the logo for the store's own shopping bags.

Fig. 10–2 The left side of the shop displays boxed kits, knitting needles, hoops, frames and display pillows. The trough above the yarn racks holds jars of buttons (beads), cotton batting, trims, crochet hooks, needles and even a basket filled with "reduced" items.

A pegboard is made by inserting a needle point through three-ply Bristol board at regular ⅛″ spacing. Board is glued to ¼″-thick balsa wood and painted. This is *later* glued onto edge of platform floor on right side (Fig. 10–4).

Plan a door and make it or purchase a door or make one from a kit. This one is a kit from Scale Model Supplies and was put together very easily. Paint finished door with prepared color. Glue door to back wall. Attach hardware.

Other areas for shelving and display purposes are planned, constructed, painted or stained, then temporarily placed in position. A small pedestal

table (Fig. 10–5) and one or two chairs are added for instruction purposes.

Create accessory items of boxes, cartons, yarn of all colors and sizes, embroidery floss, rug yarn, spools of thread, knitting needles, crochet needles, crewel and needlepoint art, kits and boxed packages of needle art, pillows, buttons, ribbons, utensils, bags, etc. These are appropriately placed around on shelves and specially constructed furniture.

There is no limit to what can be done with a needlework shop. It is a fun project in every sense of the word, but it does take time to make all the little ne-

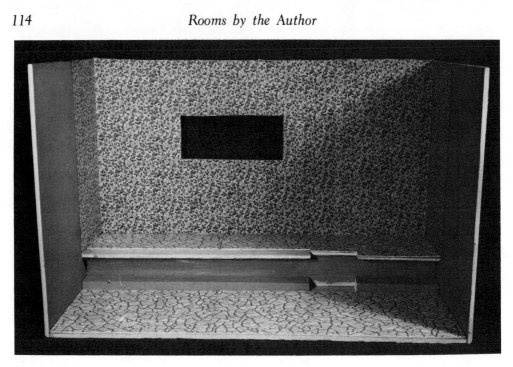

Fig. 10–3 Second-level floor is 5″ deep with a cutback area where steps are to fit in. Below, balsa wood strips ³/₈″ x 1¹/₄″ are painted and placed vertically and horizontally under second level. Again, area is cut back for step. Wall covering is applied and flooring for second level is laid down. Notice on left side that tile is set back. (Tiles cannot be cut through. They are *scored* with a sharp instrument and carefully broken apart by hand.)

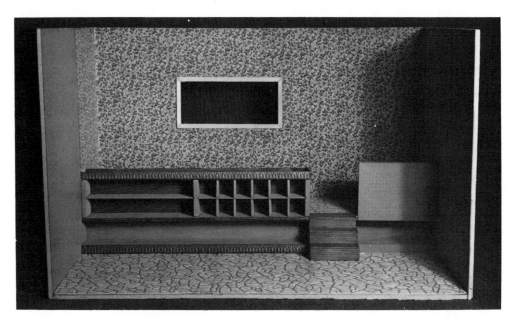

Fig. 10–4 Glass and window molding are installed. Shelves are constructed and painted, with carved trim molding added to top front and side. Strip is added to back to produce a trough which holds merchandise. Carved trim is also added to bottom. Pegboard is glued into position *after* button cards have been glued on. Steps are made, stained and glued into place.

cessities essential to a well-run miniature business.

How to Make a Ribbon Stand and Pedestal Table

Patterns and assembly techniques for these furnishings are supplied in Fig. 10–8.

Ribbon Stand

MATERIALS

Pine, $^1/_8''$ and $^3/_4''$; cocktail-size straws; dress wire hanger or plastic tubing that will fit through straw openings; narrow ribbons and laces.

DIRECTIONS

1. Cut pattern parts and stain pieces of pine wood.
2. Cut out rectangular areas in back corners of base (A), to allow bottoms of poles (B) to set in.
3. Peg bottoms of (B) for extra strength and glue onto base piece. When dry, polish.
4. Cut straws into smaller pieces. Apply glue to straw and wind small amount of ribbon around straw, continuing to apply glue as you wind.
5. After several ribbons have been wound and are dry, clip straw closer to ribbon.
6. Insert the ribbons on tubing and glue each end into bracket space.

Pedestal Table

Since spindles come in different designs, discretion by the reader will have to be used in this project. However, the finished table should measure $2^1/_2''$ high. The one in Fig. 10–5 was made according to the pattern in Fig. 10–8.

MATERIALS

Pine or walnut, $^1/_8''$ and $^1/_4''$; a turned spindle from hardware or lumber store.

DIRECTIONS

1. Stain the spindle and all wood cutout pattern pieces with walnut stain.
2. Glue spindle to center of underside of table. Allow to dry.
3. Glue three legs to bottom of spindle, proportionately spaced.
4. Polish.

Note: Cutoff top portion of *this* spindle happened to resemble a large vase, which can be painted and decorated. Flower stems can be inserted through drilled holes.

How to Make Display Cases

Plans are supplied in Figs. 10–9 and 10–10 for two styles of display cases.

First Display Case

This style has false drawers (Fig. 10–9).

MATERIALS

Pine or walnut, $^1/_{16}''$ and $^1/_{32}''$; hardware for six drawers.

DIRECTIONS

1. If wood is pine, stain all pieces.
2. Glue side pieces (C) to back piece

Fig. 10–5 The pedestal table starts with a spindle purchased at a hardware store. Part is cut off, then round top and carved legs are added. Easy, yes?

Fig. 10–6 Ribbon stand in corner of shop has beautiful ribbons ready to unwind. The rug canvas stand is made from drapery hooks and "paper clip" hangers hold assorted designs applied with colored marking pen to needlepoint canvas. The display case is waiting to be filled; note the provided selection card of embroidery floss colors. The "needlepoint" white cat is petitpoint in three colors on 18-mesh canvas.

Fig. 10–7 A wooden display case provides room for instruction books and packaged kits. The floor stand holds an assortment of needlepoint kits and two stacked napkin rings become a container for assorted needlework canvases.

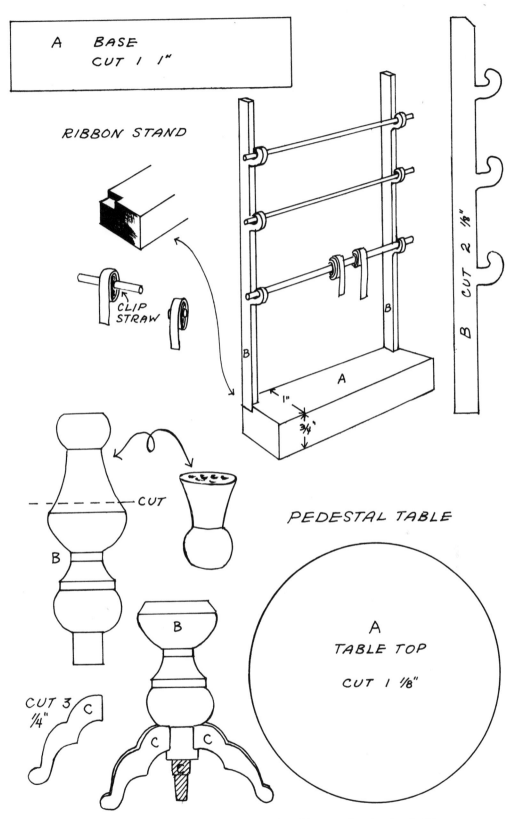

A BASE
CUT 1 1"

RIBBON STAND

CLIP STRAW

B CUT 2 ⅛"

1"

¾"

A

B

B

CUT

B

PEDESTAL TABLE

CUT 3
¼"   C

C   C

A
TABLE TOP
CUT 1 ⅛"

Fig. 10–8 Patterns and assembly guide for ribbon stand and pedestal table.

117

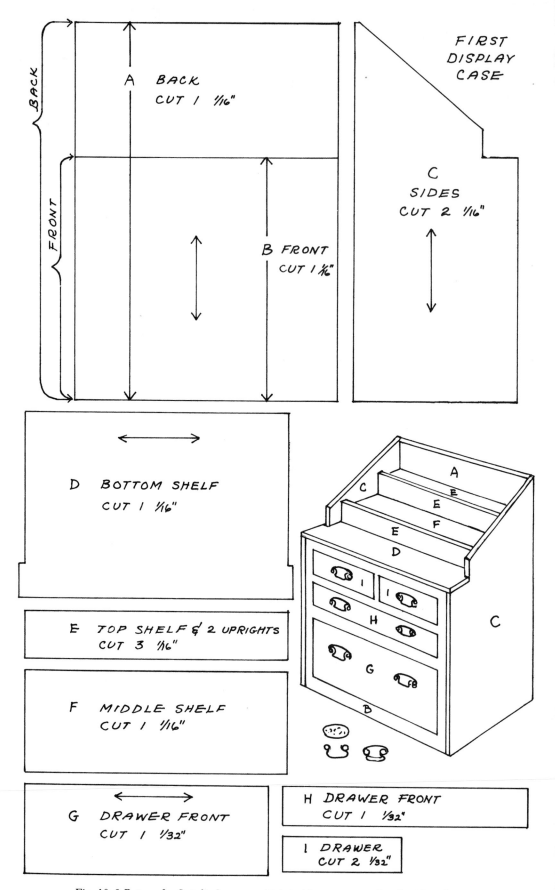

BACK

FRONT

A BACK
CUT 1 1/16"

FIRST
DISPLAY
CASE

C
SIDES
CUT 2 1/16"

B FRONT
CUT 1 1/16"

D BOTTOM SHELF
CUT 1 1/16"

E TOP SHELF & 2 UPRIGHTS
CUT 3 1/16"

F MIDDLE SHELF
CUT 1 1/16"

G DRAWER FRONT
CUT 1 1/32"

H DRAWER FRONT
CUT 1 1/32"

I DRAWER
CUT 2 1/32"

Fig. 10–9 Pattern for first display case which holds rug yarn and embroidery floss.

(A). Use graph paper to line up properly.

3. Glue front piece (B) between side pieces (C).

4. Glue first shelf (D) onto front edge of (B) and (C) and against back of (A). Be sure shelf is absolutely horizontal.

5. Glue upright (E) and second shelf (F) into place. Notice that shelf sits *lower* than top of upright.

6. Glue upright (E) and third shelf (E) into place.

7. Glue false drawers (G, H and I) to front.

8. Attach drawer pulls made from wire and escutcheon nails.

Second Display Case

The display case in Fig. 10–10 has open shelves.

MATERIALS

Pine or walnut, $1/16''$, $1/8''$ and $1/32''$.

DIRECTIONS

1. If wood is pine, stain all pieces.

2. Glue side pieces (B) to back piece (A).

3. Glue base front (D) between side pieces (B).

4. Glue base top (F) into place.

5. Glue bottom shelf (E) into place.

6. Glue middle shelf (D) into place.

7. Glue top shelf (C) into place. Glue edge (G) into place on shelf (C).

8. Glue guardrail for magazines (G) into place.

HOW TO MAKE A CANVAS STAND, KIT DISPLAY STAND AND KITS

Needlework Shop accessories are assembled as indicated in Fig. 10–11.

Canvas Stand

Two four-prong metal pleater hooks are used. This is the one with double swivel hook at top (A). Hooks and *out-side* prongs are removed. Spread two remaining prongs apart as shown in (B). Using one of the separated prongs, shape both ends into hooks (C). Using an instant-bonding glue (Krazy Glue), cement the hooks through the two end uprights as shown (C). When thoroughly dry, paint black (PLA enamel).

Rug Canvas on Hanger

Canvas is a cut piece of 12 or 14-mesh needlepoint canvas. Designs are painted on with permanent marking pens (Sharpie). Wire hangers are made from paper clips, as shown in Fig. 10–11, and canvas is glued on with folded metal pieces cut out of metal pouring spouts. Hang several designs on the canvas stand.

Kit Display Stand

A block of pine is cut to measure $1^1/4'' \times 1^1/4'' \times 3^1/2''$. Paint white. Using gluey cotton for extra holding power, glue $1^1/2''$ length of small dowel down through a nose-spray bottletop; cut through plastic with heated poultry skewer or large drapery hook. When dry, glue to large wooden button for base. Gouge out a center area underneath wooden block and glue/insert dowel securely. Paint bottom silver or black. After you have planned "needlepoint kits," cut, twist and glue/insert tiny pieces of smallest paper clips into walls of four sides of block for hooks. Glue finished kits onto hooks and block so they don't keep falling off.

Needlepoint and Crewel Kits

Kits start with a cutout color print from a needlework catalogue or magazine advertisement. Needlepoint canvas or a loosely woven fabric, stiffened with glue, is cut a bit larger. Add small

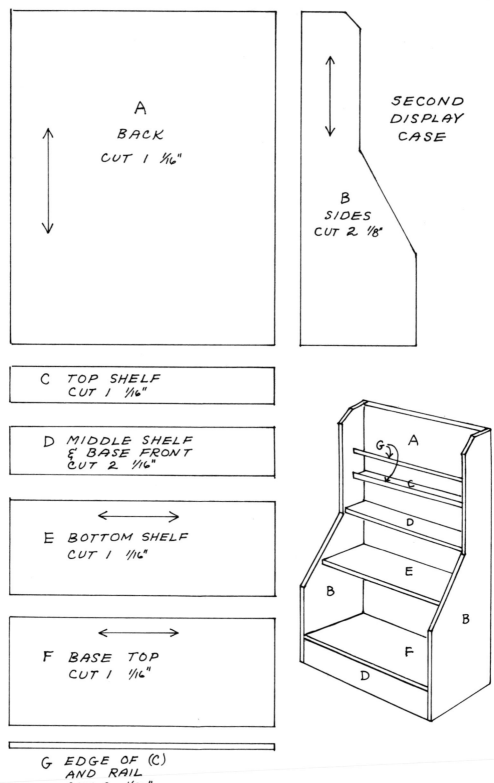

A
BACK
CUT 1 1/16"

SECOND
DISPLAY
CASE

B
SIDES
CUT 2 1/8"

C TOP SHELF
CUT 1 1/16"

D MIDDLE SHELF
& BASE FRONT
CUT 2 1/16"

E BOTTOM SHELF
CUT 1 1/16"

F BASE TOP
CUT 1 1/16"

G EDGE OF (C)
AND RAIL
CUT 2 1/32"

Fig. 10–10 Pattern for second display case which holds instructions, magazines and boxed kits.

120

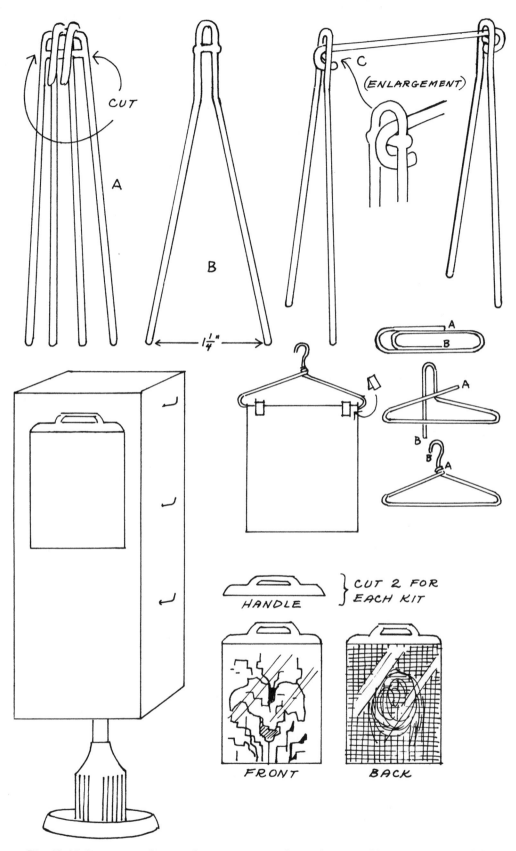

Fig. 10–11 Construction drawings for rug canvas stand, wire hanger and kit display stand with kits.

strands of embroidery floss. Wrap every-thing in cellophane. Glue ends closed with Duco Cement. Glue double handle, cut from card, to top.

How to Make Needlework Accessories

An assortment of finished projects and raw materials is shown in Fig. 10–12. Procedures for making these accessories are illustrated in Fig. 10–13.

Skeins of Yarn

Wind one strand of Persian yarn several times around a piece of card. Slip off and wrap a strip of white or black Mystik tape around center area. Close with spot of glue. Cut off two loose threads close to tape. For larger skeins, cut card wider.

Rug Yarn

Stretch one 20″ strand of Persian yarn on waxed paper. Brush with diluted white glue to stiffen. Remove to another clean sheet of waxed paper to dry. When dry, cut into ¹/₂″ pieces (A). Stack pieces together (B). Wrap Mystik tape around center very tightly (C). Close tape with spot of glue. With sharp scissors cut away excess yarn, leaving small amount showing as in drawing (D). Do several of these at the same time with wide selection of colors.

Embroidery Floss

Cut 2″ length of acetate, about ¹/₂″ wide. Apply white glue to *both* sides of acetate. Carefully wind embroidery floss around acetate, keeping floss *even and straight*. Do not overlap in a zigzag fashion. When dry, carefully cut away about every two sections of floss. With black inkpen, stripe in two markings for wrapping. Make several at the same time in different colors.

Floss Selection Chart

Use a needle to punch holes in card about ¹/₈″ apart. Cut several pieces of different colors. Pull off two strands from each color. Fold, insert and pull through each two strands, as shown in Fig. 10–13. Cut all floss even across bottom when finished.

Thread

Fine threads are wound around a small rice bead, or small cut pieces of tiny dowel are grooved in the center and thread is wound around; tack with glue.

Hoops

Hoops are made from links; some are cut and squeezed smaller and placed within larger size. Oval is cut from pull-off tab of single-size juice can. Large round is a spiral from notebook or check book, cut apart.

Boxes

Brown packaging boxes are drawn onto *very heavy* brown grocery bags. Two sizes of 1″ and 1¹/₂″ are denoted by length of arrows in Fig. 10–13. Ends are pulled up and glued. Stuff with yarn.

Needlepoint Wall Clock

For a special clock, petitpoint a pansy in three colors on 18-mesh canvas. Cut out hands from metal; add head of straight pin for pivot.

White Cat and Turtle Needlepoints

Use 18-mesh canvas and petitpoint designs with colors appropriate for the picture.

Fig. 10–12 Some of the items that outfit the Needlework Shop are arranged and displayed. The turtle on a lily pad is petitpoint. The large panel of embroidery is a cut portion of a handkerchief, padded and framed. Of the three pillows, the round one is cut out of embroidery material; the oblong on the left is made from ribbon trim which resembles bargello; the square pillow is made from patchwork trim for which the Seminole Indians are remarkably talented. The lovely tan and brown granny afghan was made by Donna Murray. All other accessories are described in the text.

Latch Hook

Shape handle out of toothpick. Twist end of straight pin back on itself. Cut shorter and glue/insert into handle.

Needles and Crochet Hooks

Glue piece of black bias tape onto card. Glue a few cut ends of straight pins onto tape. Glue a few longer pieces of cut straight pins with bent ends onto

tape. Cut away excess areas. Cut acetate to fit over top. Use black Mystik tape and, adhering small amount on front edge, extend over back area and around to other front side. Cut off excess.

Buttons

Several pieces of card are cut to size shown. Buttons are seed beads, rocaille beads, bugle beads, ends of pins

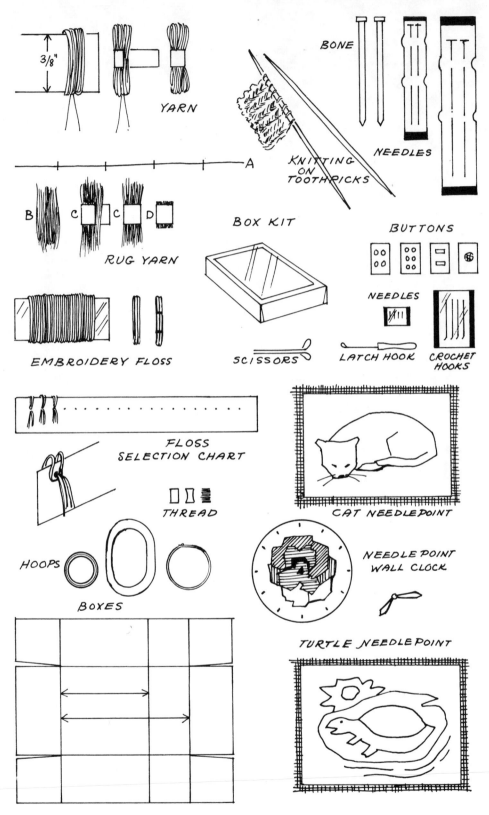

Fig. 10–13 Construction drawings for needlework accessories.

124

(straight and round heads) rhinestones, sequins and any doodad small enough to qualify. Make arrangements of several of same bead in different colors.

Box Kit

Cut out designs from catalogues and advertisements. Cut pieces of balsa or pine wood larger than cutout and about $1/8''$ or $3/16''$ deep. Paint "box" white or sides can be black or red. Glue picture on top. Wrap in cellophane and glue ends closed.

Scissors and Needles

Purchase miniature scissors or make out of sewing hooks, as shown in Fig. 10–13. To make needles, two different-size pins are colored red and blue with permanent marking pen (Sharpie) and inserted through white card holders, as shown in Fig. 10–13. Wrap up in cellophane.

Knitting Supplies

Bone needles are cut round toothpicks. The ends are bluntly pointed and tops have thin slices of tiny dowel glued on. Paint white.

Using Persian yarn or crochet yarn, knit a small length with round toothpicks. Carefully remove toothpick and insert bone needle, described above.

Other items which are in the room or suggestions to be added are rolled needlepoint canvas, finished pillows, foam pillow forms, mini frames, quilt batting, quilt hoops, designer pillowcases, knit case with needles, knitting bag with stand, sewing baskets, shopping bags with store logo, etc.

Those who knit or crochet will want to make a scarf, stole, shawl, vest, poncho, afghan, bedspread, etc., to display in the shop.

One thing about doing a needlework shop . . . you're never really finished.

CHAPTER
11

The Belle of Amherst Setting

The Belle of Amherst was a remarkable one-woman show in which Julie Harris portrayed Emily Dickinson. Awaiting the performance, I had the good fortune to be sitting in the front row and since the curtain was already pulled back, the set was fully exposed. As I was hypnotized by this very simple, lovely arrangement, my pen began to slither across the program, creating sketches of furnishings and fine touches. Julie's performance cinched it! I knew I had to do the set in miniature, which reinforces my theory that inspiration can strike at the most unexpected times.

How to Complete the Set

True to the actual set, this miniature rendition is finished in its simplest form (Fig. 11–1 and color section, Figs. 8 and 9). A mere fragment of velvet instills the effect of drapery and the simple backdrop of silhouetted tree shapes (as seen in the traveling company) are the only features designating a stage setting.

All furniture and accessories, exemplary of the era in which Emily Dickinson is portrayed, are duplicated as closely as possible in both style and color scheme. A writing table, a French armchair, a tea cart and a red Victorian sofa are the principal furniture pieces in the foreground. The back of the stage includes a white iron bed, a melodeon covered with mementoes and pictures, and the proverbial hat and umbrella stand complete with white straw bonnet, checkered cape and parasol. Other little necessities, such as a chest, boxes and sewing basket, are appropriately placed, as are all the proper social items on table, tea cart and writing table.

All furniture is created out of hardwoods—walnut, cherry, mahogany or pine, stained to resemble the master piece. Some of the accessories are handmade or contrived, while others are necessarily purchases.

The "iron" bed is actually made of hardwood and the bedspread is made from worn pajamas, a lightweight material, that was dyed tan with a tea solution (Fig. 11–3).

The small parquet box in front (Fig. 11–4) is achieved by laying on different stains of color. Each stain is mixed with a very *small* amount of white glue, which prevents bleeding. As each stain color dries, the next application of color is carefully brushed on.

126

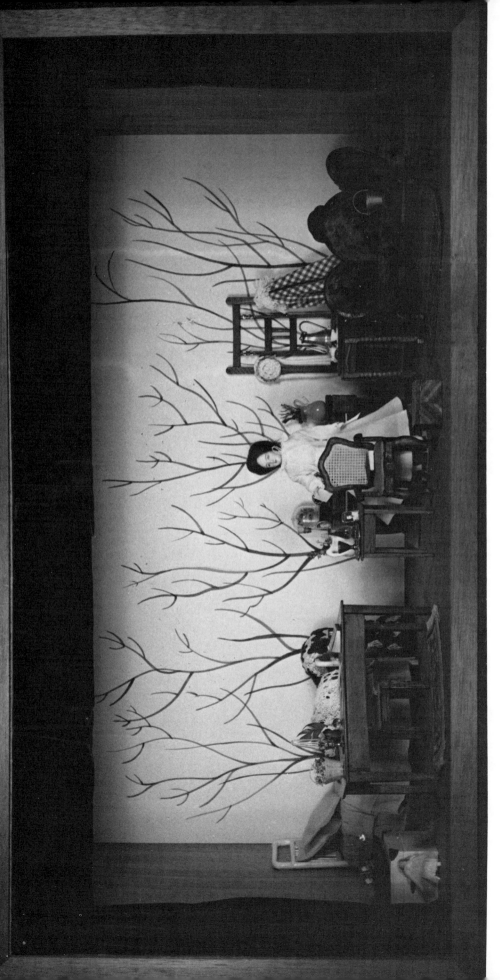

Fig. 11–1 A memorable evening is preserved in miniature. *The Belle of Amherst*, starring Julie Harris and deservedly a winner, is duplicated in an unusual and beautiful room, 24″ wide. An in-teresting array of furnishings reminiscent of the Victorian era is presented, along with all the little accessories and mementoes that personalize the set.

Fig. 11–2 Another view of *The Belle of Amherst* set in miniature.

Fig. 11–3 The "iron" bed is made out of hardwood, dowels and antiseptic sticks. A granny afghan is laid atop a ruffled spread with pillow shams; a small one-inch doll rests against a gray painted chest.

Fig. 11–4 Special pieces of furniture include a French armchair with "cane" back, small Victorian sofa, umbrella stand, a mahogany storage box and small parquet box. Directions are given in text. The lovely doll who becomes our star was made by Ann Brown of Racketty-Packetty Dolls and was dressed by the author in white batiste, trimmed with lace and satin belt.

Portraits of "family" are miniature pictures of my own family and other little accessories are best described with the directions and drawings that follow.

Although all the pieces of furniture are interesting, only a few are described in detail with patterns provided (Fig. 11–4). Any or all can be used in other room settings of your choice.

How to Make a Victorian Umbrella Stand

Pattern parts and assembly guide are provided in Fig. 11–5.

MATERIALS

Pine or walnut, $1/16''$, $1/8''$ and $7/8''$; miniature hooks.

DIRECTIONS

1. Tape waxed paper over graph paper. This helps to line up joints properly. The back part of stand will be laid flat onto waxed and graph paper (steps 3–7) for positioning and gluing.

2. Stain *all* pieces of pine wood with walnut stain.

3. Glue pieces (B) to base (A).

4. Glue pieces (C) to base (A).

5. Glue pieces (G) and (H) to base (A) and between other vertical pieces (C) and (B). Set back slightly.

6. Glue pieces (D) and (E) into place.

7. Measure and cut two round toothpicks (F) to fit. Stain and glue in place.

8. Glue front posts (I) into place. Glue cross pieces (J) and (K) into place.

9. Polish the wood or varnish with polyurethane.

10. Add hooks.

How to Make a Storage Box

Fig. 11–6 provides pattern parts and assembly guide for the storage box.

129

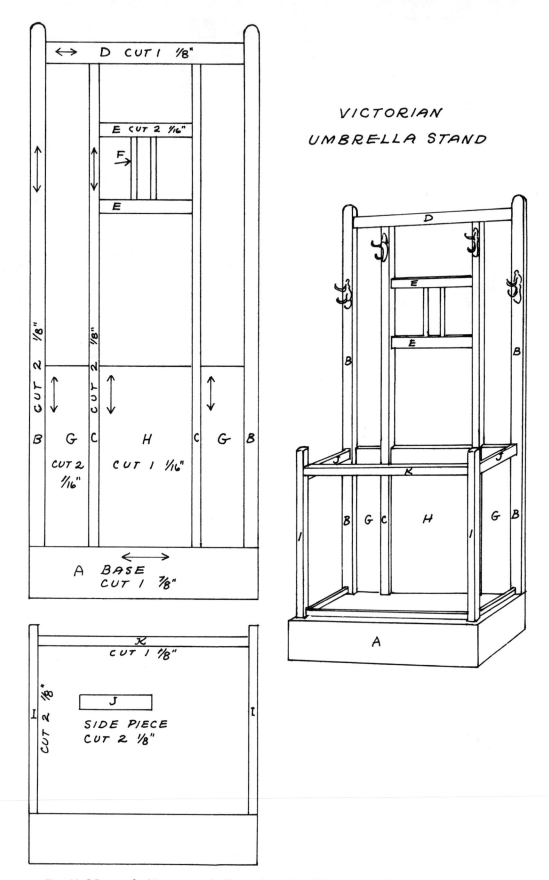

Fig. 11–5 Pattern for Victorian umbrella stand, a nice additional piece for any Victorian home.

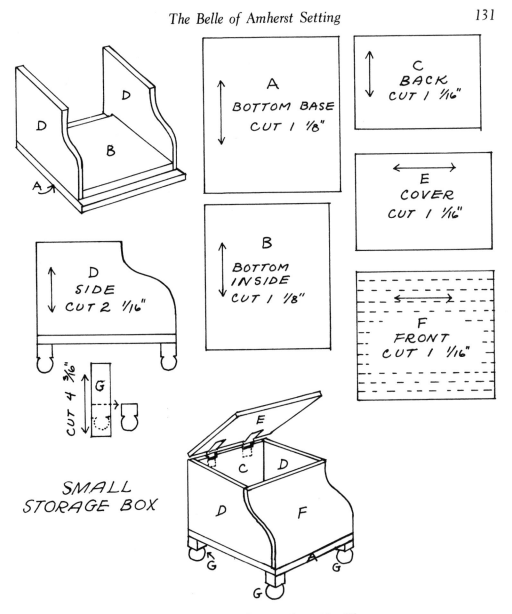

Fig. 11–6 Pattern for small storage box with a lift-up top.

MATERIALS

Mahogany, $1/16''$, $1/8''$ and $3/16''$; two square hinges.

DIRECTIONS

1. Glue inside base piece (B) onto bottom base piece (A), *centering* it.

2. Glue two side pieces (D) and back piece (C) onto bottom pieces (A) and (B), and against each other at back.

3. With metal-edge ruler and knife,

cut front piece (F) into several $1/8''$ or smaller slices. *Be sure to keep them in order as each cut is made.*

4. Starting at top of box front, individually glue down *each* strip, piece by piece, adjusting to the curve of the sides. (Bending the wood with steam or boiling water did not soften it enough to respond to a tight curve; hence this method is used.)

5. When front area is dry, sand away any rough spots, obtaining a nice curvature.

6. Carve a ball on all four legs of (G). When satisfied, cut the leg down to size indicated in Fig. 11–6. Glue onto four corners of bottom (A).

7. Position hinges on top piece (E) and back piece (C). Cut out two small sections in top of (C) for hinge insertion and glue hinges to *outside* of back (C) and *inside* of top (E).

8. Sand piece well with fine sandpaper, stain and finish with Minwax.

How to Make a Victorian Sofa

Figs. 11–7 and 11–8 supply parts and assembly techniques for the miniature Victorian sofa.

MATERIALS

Walnut, $1/16''$, $1/8''$, $3/16''$ and $1/4''$; $3/16''$ dowel; three-ply Bristol board; fine velvet material for upholstery; masking tape; art foam.

DIRECTIONS

1. Because of narrow edging strips, back piece (A) is cut in two pieces and later glued together. The two back pieces are soaked in boiled water until flexible enough to bend around a curved object to approximate curve of seat (D). I used a small stainless-steel bowl, as shown in Fig. 11–9. Tape securely to your shaping object until well dried.

2. Glue two pieces (A) together, matching at center. Add some strong tape over the glued areas for extra security, but not to the top—only where upholstery will cover. Dry well.

3. Glue extra curved piece (C) to top of sofa and glue piece (B) above (A) and (C).

4. Sand and round the front area of seat (D).

5. Glue seat (D) to bottom of back piece (A). See Fig. 11–8.

6. Cut upholstery material $3/8''$ larger than (I) and (H) and cover each card,

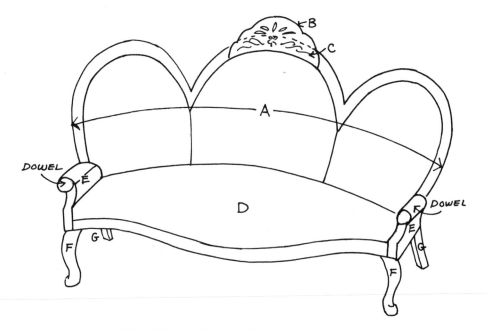

Fig. 11–7 Assembly guide for small Victorian sofa.

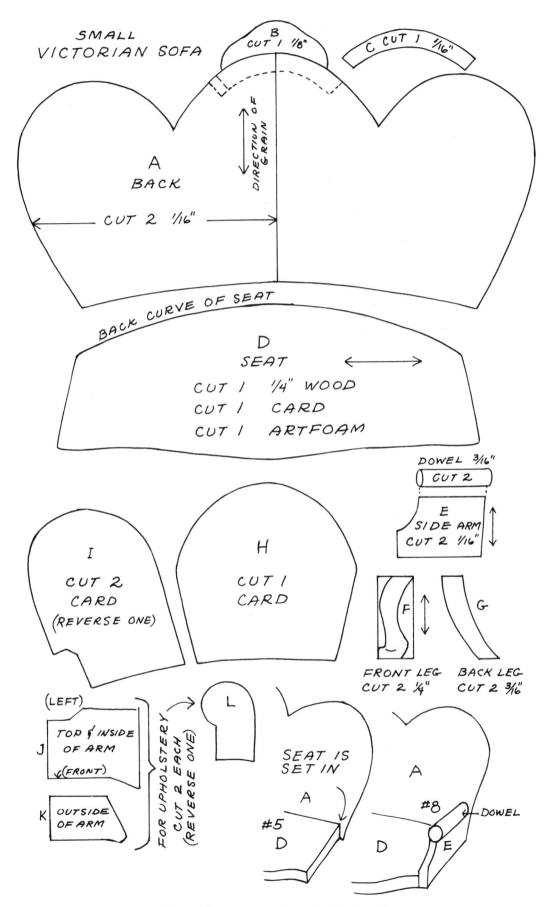

SMALL VICTORIAN SOFA

B CUT 1 1/8"

C CUT 1 1/16"

DIRECTION OF GRAIN

A
BACK
CUT 2 1/16"

BACK CURVE OF SEAT

D
SEAT
CUT 1   1/4" WOOD
CUT 1   CARD
CUT 1   ARTFOAM

DOWEL 3/16"
CUT 2

E
SIDE ARM
CUT 2 1/16"

I
CUT 2
CARD
(REVERSE ONE)

H
CUT 1
CARD

F

G

FRONT LEG
CUT 2 1/4"

BACK LEG
CUT 2 3/16"

(LEFT)

J   TOP & INSIDE
    OF ARM
    (FRONT)

L

FOR UPHOLSTERY
CUT 2 EACH
(REVERSE ONE)

K   OUTSIDE
    OF ARM

SEAT IS
SET IN

A

#5

D

A

#8

DOWEL

D

E

Fig. 11–8 Pattern parts for small Victorian sofa.

Fig. 11–9 Wooden back pieces for Victorian sofa are soaked in very hot water and taped to a curved surface, in this case a stainless-steel bowl.

inserting cotton for padding. Pull the material around to back of card and glue. Try for fit on sofa. These should be snug. Do not glue down yet.

7. Sand smooth and curve top area of sofa back; rout out a design on pieces (B) and (C).

8. Glue side arms (E) into place and glue dowel on top, making any necessary adjustments. See Fig. 11–7.

9. Cover arms of sofa with upholstery material, starting with piece (L); glue and trim. Next, apply piece (J) and then piece (K).

10. Cut material for card (D) $^3/_8''$ larger and cover seat card and art foam. Glue to back of card.

11. Try upholstered seat and back on sofa together for snug fit. Make any necessary adjustments. When satisfied, glue all four pieces down.

12. On back of sofa, cut out material to cover, leaving $^1/_8''$ of wood showing around the three curved areas, but bring material down even with bottom of seat.

13. Carve two front cabriole legs (F). Shape and sand well.

14. Shape and sand back legs (G).

15. Glue all four legs into position. These can be pegged in place, using the directions given for the legs of French armchair.

How to Make a French Armchair

Patterns and assembly guide for the chair are supplied in Fig. 11–11.

MATERIALS

Walnut, $^1/_8''$, $^3/_{16}''$, $^1/_4''$ and $^3/_8''$; three-ply Bristol board; art foam; fabric of thin velvet; 12-mesh needlepoint canvas.

Fig. 11–10 Wooden skeleton construction of Victorian sofa and padded velvet sections ready to be glued onto wooden structure.

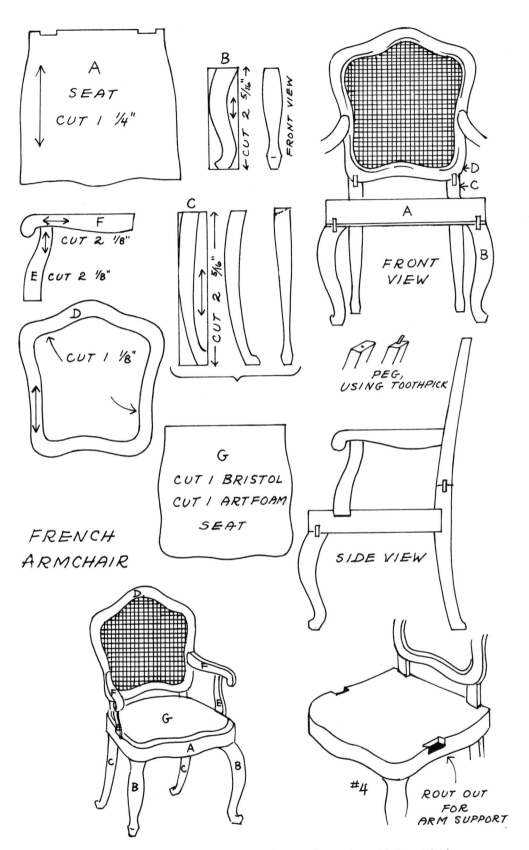

A SEAT CUT 1 ¼"

B ← CUT 2 5/16" → FRONT VIEW

F CUT 2 ⅛"

E CUT 2 ⅛"

C ← CUT 2 5/16" →

D CUT 1 ⅛"

G CUT 1 BRISTOL CUT 1 ARTFOAM SEAT

FRENCH ARMCHAIR

FRONT VIEW

PEG, USING TOOTHPICK

SIDE VIEW

#4 ROUT OUT FOR ARM SUPPORT

Fig. 11–11 Pattern and assembly guide for French armchair with "cane" back.

DIRECTIONS

1. Shape the two front cabriole legs (B), using knife, Dremel Moto-Tool and needle files.

2. Shape the two back legs (C).

3. Gently sand all edges of piece (A) on sides and front for slight curvature.

4. With razor blade, rout out areas on both sides of seat (A) as shown on side view drawing (1/8″ down and 1/16″ inward).

5. Finish sanding and rounding necessary edges of pieces (E) and (F), and *front* edges of (D).

6. Prepare tops of legs (B) for gluing to seat bottom (A) by pegging with toothpicks. See Fig. 11–11. Rout out hole; insert glue and toothpick; dry; clip toothpick, leaving small amount; again rout out hole on bottom of seat; add glue and insert toothpick and secure leg against surface. Dry well. Angled corner will be sanded and rounded later.

7. Glue two back legs into back cut-out areas of seat (A). Dry well.

8. Tops of legs (C) will have to be cut and curved to accommodate back piece (D).

9. When satisfied with fit, prepare tops of back legs (C) for pegging and joining (D), as in previous directions. Glue; dry well.

10. Try arm support pieces (E) for fit into seat groove on sides. Correct if necessary. Glue into place.

11. Try arm pieces (F) for fit. Adjust back of arm for any slant and shorten arm if necessary. Glue to pieces (E) and (D).

12. When all joints are well dried, round and refine all areas of seat, legs, arms, etc. Use Moto-Tool, needle files and fine sandpaper.

13. Cover Bristol board cutout (G) with 1/8″ art foam.

14. Snugly cover form, topping with thin velvet material; pull material around to underside of cardboard and glue well.

15. Stain chair. Polish with Minwax (except seat).

16. With acrylic paint, color a piece of needlepoint canvas either cream or ochre. Cut out to fit open center of back (D). Glue into area.

17. Securely glue velvet seat down onto seat (A).

How to Make an Iron Bed and Set Accessories

Fig. 11–12 provides pattern parts and assembly techniques for *The Belle of Amherst* setting.

White "Iron" Bed

Toothpick pegs (see Fig. 2–4) are inserted within corner shape pieces (A). Insert other end of pegs into 3/16″-dowel crossbars and upright pieces (B). Carve, shape and sand four corner pieces to a curved shape (C), matching dowel width.

Cut crossbar dowels *slightly* wider. Curve end areas with round needle file (D). Glue into place between upright pieces.

Cut applicator sticks slightly longer for upright bars on head and foot of bed. Sand ends, curving inward, and glue snugly into place.

Paint entire structure with PLA white enamel model paint. Attach headboard and footboard with sides and a bottom and fit with a mattress.

Parquet Box

This is a display piece; it does not open. Cut block out of hard pine, 1 1/8″ x 3/4″ x 3/4″. With sharp-pointed instrument and file, incise an indentation

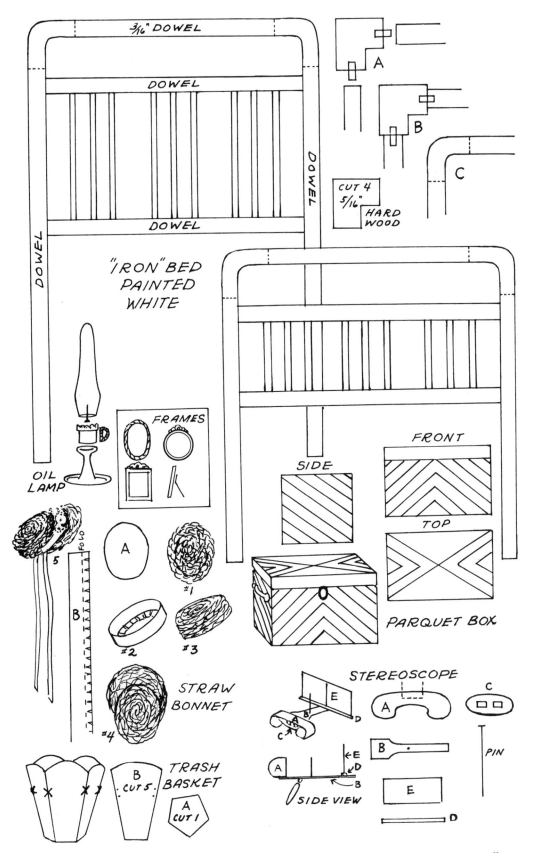

Fig. 11–12 Plans and construction guide for white "iron" bed, parquet box, oil lamp, small frames, straw bonnet, trash basket and stereoscope.

1/8″ down from top *all around block*.
See Fig. 11–12. Sand block smooth.

Lightly detail striped areas on block
with pencil. Apply clear stain and sealer. When dry, apply a medium color
stain to *some* stripes. When dry, apply a
darker color stain to other stripes. *Note*:
Stains are mixed with a little white
glue, as described in Ch. 3.

Oil Lamp

There are different ways to arrive at
an oil lamp, but this one is made from
an ampule (or large, clear capsule), cutoff small nail, metal finding, metal shirt
stud and cut filigree.

Frames

A variety of small frames are contrived from oval and round links from
jewelry chains, nail heads and metal
edging, shaped into a square. Aluminum stand is cut, bent and glued to
back after small snapshots taken of old
family photographs have been glued
into frame area. Cut filigree can be
added to top.

Straw Bonnet

A flexible braid is needed for working
this project. I used thin orange raffia
from an orange bag and plaited the long
strands. Another substitute for straw is
Persian yarn, slightly coated with white
glue and plaited.

1. Starting in center of piece (A),
wind and glue braided strand around
and around to meet outer edge.

2. Glue piece (B) to underside of
piece (A). Dry.

3. Glue braided strand around outside of piece (B). Thrice around should
be sufficient.

4. Glue braided strands, starting at
front of hat, to form peak. Add on accordingly, shaping and cutting. Dry.
Paint everything white with PLA
enamel model paint.

5. Add a thin white ribbon around
front and sides of brim, dropping excess
down from sides for tie. Add petite
flowers on top of glued ribbon. I used
the smallest dried wildflowers for a most
delicate touch.

Trash Basket

Cut pattern for the five-sided basket
out of three-ply Bristol board. Punch
four holes in each piece (B), as indicated, with a sharp needle. Glue lower
part of each piece (B) onto piece (A),
gluing sides together one by one. When
thoroughly dry, paint with brown paint
and white glue mixture. Using brown
button thread, catch through the
punched holes with a crisscross stitch
on the outside.

Stereoscope

Flat pieces (A, B, C, D, E) are cut
out of card. Curve both ends of piece
(A) under and glue onto end of wide
edge of piece (B). Glue piece (C) onto
back curved opening of piece (A). Glue
piece (D) across piece (B). Glue straight
pin into (B), indicated by dot. Dry well.

Clip off protruding bottom area and
upper area (see side view in Fig.
11–12). Paint everything brown, including piece (E). Glue a pair of *matching* black and white pictures onto piece
(E) and glue onto crossbar piece (D).
Duplicate copies of catalogues provide a
good source of picture material. Add a
small handle to bottom: brown rice
bead can be used.

CHAPTER
12

The Mystery Room

What pops into your head when the word *gallery* is mentioned? Art gallery? Photographic gallery? Sculpture gallery? Antique gallery? Auction gallery? Theater gallery?

These were some of the thoughts that passed through my mind as I prepared to finish off the "staircase room" in Fig. 12–1.

And then my husband had to go and spoil it all. He said he didn't see it as a gallery at all. With a vivid imagination, he described a castle room, a haunted house room, a movie set or (horrors!) a hangman's execution chamber.

Now I had second thoughts!

But then a new idea occurred to me. Why finish the room? Why not let the reader finish it in his own inimitable way? Much of the groundwork has already been laid in information and imagination, and whatever pops into your mind when you glance at the "staircase room" can become another whole story in itself.

If anyone sees any merit in this project and feels challenged, this can be a great fun experiment . . . especially for groups.

So I'm asking you! How would *you* finish off the walls, the floor, the ceiling?

What would you do to the staircase? Make it simple or elaborate? Would you use wood balusters and handrails or improvise something resembling iron, screen, rope or mesh? Would the stairs be painted, stained, marbleized or covered with a runner of lush red velvet or some other covering?

How about that arched window? Would you use clear, frosted or stained glass, or something else innovative and new? A special pictorial glass related to *your* special room could be outstanding.

Doors! Should any be added for extra interest and mystery? Doors on the first floor mean one thing, but doors on the balcony floor can imply something (?) else. The balcony needs some planning. Should it be shortened on the side walls, eliminated on one wall or abbreviated to only the back wall? And how will it be supported? Must pillars be used or will a buttress construction be adequate? A stringer staircase needs no extra support, but if you want to add a decorative flourish in this area, be imaginative.

Fig. 12–1 Front view of the Mystery Room shows an interesting staircase and landing, a wrap-around balcony and an arched window. This is the shell of a room intended to be imaginatively finished off by the reader.

There's that fascinating niche under the stair landing. What an excellent place for a fountain, lush garden arrangement, sculpture, lavish art d'objet, showcase or some other intriguing showpiece.

How about giant-size murals and plush hanging drapery with tassels and trim? Do they fit into your scheme of things?

Lighting fixtures can be simple, dramatic or elegant. Spotlight "something" under that stair landing or hang a sumptuous chandelier smack in the middle of the room. Indirect lighting can poke rays of illumination from under the balcony; wall fixtures, tried and true, are always in good taste.

The particulars of this box room are very simple. It is almost square in appearance. The dimensions are 20″ wide, 18″ high and 16″ deep. The stringer stairs, which are individual stairs glued together, are made by Carlson's Miniatures. I like their strong appearance, as well as their easy construction method. The basic construction wood used, including the balcony, is ¼″ birch plywood, but any plywood is acceptable. The balcony measures 4¹/₂″

Fig. 12–2 A more sinister view of the Mystery Room shows the dramatic climb of the staircase and landing, a challenging project to complete.

deep all around the arched window, cut out of the back, is 2″ wide and 6″ high. An astute reader will notice that the floor has been covered with vinyl tile that resembles marble, but that was done in a moment of weakness before this project culminated in the Mystery Room.

Well, what are you waiting for? Let's see what *you* can do!

PART III

Rooms by
Guest Miniaturists

*A hobby is something a man does, not because
he thinks he should or because someone else
wants him to, but because he likes doing it.
. . . You don't have to do it well for it to be a
hobby. You only have to enjoy it.*

HANNAH LEES (1904–)

CHAPTER
13

A Picture Gallery

Whenever I think of miniaturists and the vast number involved, as compared to a few years ago, I feel a warm glow. This remarkable hobby is enjoyed by so many different people of varied talents. There are enthusiastic young adults just starting out and mature individuals who boast of years and years of experienced collecting and crafting. Some people work as individuals and others have dual relationships of marriage and "miniature" businesses. Correspondence opens the way for new friendships and an exciting new life awaits many who embark upon the Lilliputian path.

The direction that miniaturists take is determined by talent and special interests. Artisans with vast experience reduce their abilities to minute size, producing remarkably beautiful small products. Miniaturists with assurance provide guidance and enlightenment through workshop programs and others become the constant collectors, ever searching and ever buying to satisfy their own needs for miniature possessions.

Escape into the Lilliputian world takes place through a variety of meth-

ods. Those who create rooms may use the talents of others or, if they are self-endowed, will produce their very own renditions. A room may exemplify an individual's handmade furnishings completely designed, planned and created by that single person. Another miniaturist, through the use of available printed plans, may also make his own furnishings by hand or augment them by the use of kits, thereby achieving a feeling similar to a hand-crafted article. Still other miniaturists, devoid of time and talent (although I sometimes question the latter), will gleefully furnish their rooms with purchases, making use of artisans' skills and manufactured products. No matter how one goes about creating his room, the final concept will still portray the individual enthusiasm of the involved miniaturist.

This chapter includes the work of a small segment of miniaturists, representing a varied selection of talents, dreams and accomplishments. For some, miniaturing is a chapter in the book of life. For others, it has become almost a life-long career. From a talented young lady to dedicated couples to a mature grandfather who's been collecting and crafting for many, many years, we see examples of tiny work: all different, exciting and beautiful to behold.

Will miniaturing endure? If integrity and perseverance prevail, it will. If knowledge and perception of proper value are upheld, it will. If creativity is encouraged and expanded, it will. But more than anything, if the right to happiness and therapeutic benefits are fully realized, it will remain an endearing and enduring hobby.

Fig. 13–1 Norman Forgue, who has created more than 100 miniature rooms, presents his rendition of a Toy Shop. Between 300 and 400 items are displayed in a brightly illuminated built-in box room. The back case is made from inlaid wood and the packages, representing kits and toys, are covered in papers dis-playing their contents. The round table in the foreground turns at 1 rpm when switch is activated. Thin strips of wood at front of case give the illusion of a storefront without interfering with the view. (*Larry DeVera, photograph*)

Fig. 13–2 The Soldier Shop is a free-standing, complete structure with large windows and sloping roof. Glass cases have sliding door backs. Equipped with indirect lighting, this amazing shop was made by Norman Forgue. (*Larry De-Vera, photograph*)

Fig. 13–3 The view through the front window of the Soldier Shop shows figures ranging in size from 7/8″ to 1 1/4″. Each is hand painted, as was its larger counterpart, which required about 100 hours of painting time by Norman Forgue. Tanks and military equipment share space with the miniature soldiers which are dressed suitably for different eras of history. All fronts for cases are friction fitted and lift out by simply pulling the decorative handles at top of window. (*Larry DeVera, photograph*)

Fig. 13-4 Norman Forgue's collection includes the Grocery Store, complete with packaged items, fresh baked goods and excellent produce. Watermelons are made from painted hazelnuts. Grandma looks over the fruits and vegetables, all handmade by Mr. Forgue, as are the small berry boxes and cases. (*Larry DeVera, photograph*)

Fig. 13–5 Sally and Wayne Lasch created a thoroughly restful Garden Room, devoid of clutter. The background scene is a Japanese garden picture from a calendar. A gravel walk, bushes, a sundial and a small garden with a statue fill in the area between the picture and the glass windows. There are two small lights between picture and windows near the floor. Using pots and shells for containers, Sally purchased some of the plants and made others from air fern, Pendo and plastic greens. The fountain on the left wall was made as follows: The base is a shell put in plaster of paris in a round container. When dry, outside was covered with plastic stone sheet from Holgae and Reynolds. The back is made from heavy cardboard covered with the same plastic stone and decorated with polyester appliques from Unique Miniatures. A shell was glued to the back. The two shells were filled with casting resin for "water." The bottom shell contains clear plastic fish, painted orange, small shells and small pieces of plastic plants. The waterfall was made with Scotch tape. Clever, indeed! The floor is real slate. Other incidentals include a brightly colored flowered hanging light, white "wicker" furniture and knickknacks and books in a bookcase inset (right wall) from Unique Miniatures. (Wayne Lasch, photograph)

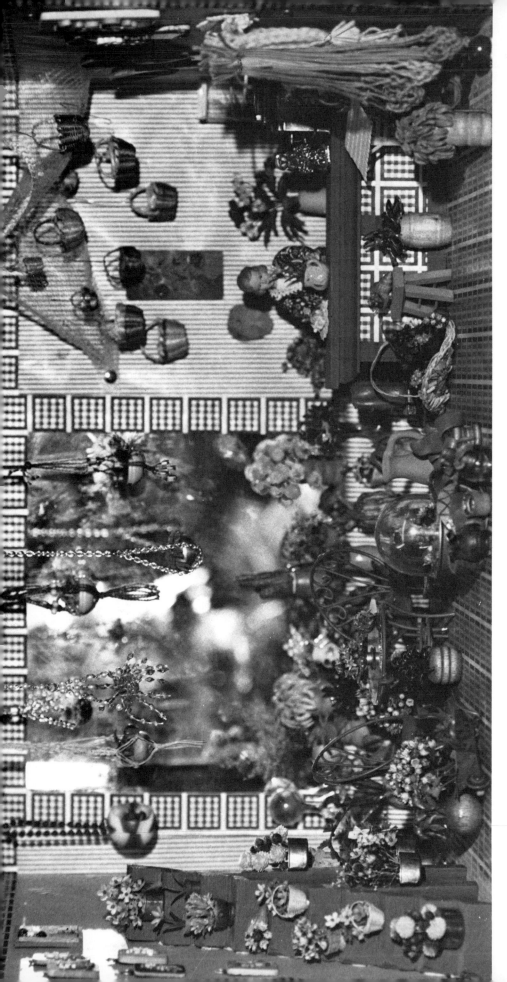

Fig. 13-6 Plants breathe life into a miniature room. The Garden Shop by Deborah Murray Couch is busy with a vast selection of handmade creations ranging from bread-dough plants to dried flower arrangements. Deborah also created macrame hangers from crochet string, beads and combinations of both. Quilled flower arrangements adorn the walls and basket arrangements are interestingly placed on a stepladder-like structure on left side. Planters are beads, baskets and some hand-molded pots. (*Norman Pollock, photograph*)

Fig. 13-7 Toy shops seem to be irresistible. Deborah Murray Couch offers her rendition. The feminine approach is apparent with the perky ruffled, tiered curtains, made from shirred trim. The neatly displayed toys are mostly commercial plastic items. The wee dollhouse, games and trimmed shelf structures are made by Deborah. (*Norman Pollock, photograph*)

Fig. 13–8 Peter Westcott, who teaches classes in miniature construction and interior decoration were accomplished by Anne struction, designed and built this lovely paneled room complete Haig and Elizabeth Kinsey. The room, which is a Williamsburg with window-seat arrangement and built-in bookcase. The room creation, is decorated in the simple Christmas style which was measures 22″ wide by 11″ deep by 10″ high. The furniture con- typical of that time. (*Peter Westcott, photograph*)

Fig. 13–10 Rosanne Chilcoat finished off the interior of her room with a charming Christmas scene. A decorated tree, wreath and toys symbolically tell their story as Santa peers around the corner. (*Peter Westcott, photograph*)

Fig. 13–9 A small box room includes the basic techniques for dollhouse construction, as taught by Peter Westcott. Rosanne Chilcoat constructed this box, leaving one side and the top visible and protected with plastic. (*Peter Westcott, photograph*)

Fig. 13–11 Anneruth Pfister is another quiet talent who has accomplished much with miniature rooms. In her old-time Pottery Shop, over 230 pieces of pottery—all made by Anneruth from her own molds—are hand painted and glazed in a variety of designs and shapes. As a young girl, she was in such a shop in Germany and has jammed the interior from top to floor with interesting merchandise, as she remembers its full-size counterpart. The proprietor is an antique doll with hand-painted features, cleverly made and costumed with felt material.

Fig. 13–12 An Oriental shop titled Eastern Bazaar was constructed from produce boxes. Using her skills with ceramic work, Anneruth Pfister created and painted. The left and right sides are angled, producing a rather open molds for ceramic sculptured work and other Oriental art objects. Hanging appearance. The same boxes were also made into square tables; round wall rugs are from old cigarette packages and the two lovely Oriental dolls lacquered tables were cut from small bouillon cube containers, designed are very old and very appropriate in this room.

Fig. 13–13 The Village Store room is filled with pottery pieces of kitchenware, tableware and more, all made by Anneruth Pfister. The Shaker family and barrels are also created from molds. The food is shaped, painted and properly displayed on platters.

Fig. 13–14 Needlework is a talent of Marilyn Forbes. She transforms a room constructed by her husband into a prize-winning Quilting Bee room. The four quilts on the back wall are copies of full-size quilts and a fifth one is being worked on by four corn- husk dolls. All quilts, rugs, pillows and hens on nests (upper top left) were made by Marilyn. Rolls of fabric are wound on bolts within a wall stand on the right side and other supplies are stored on the left wall shelving.

Fig. 13–15 Constructed by Thomas Forbes, an old-time saloon is imaginatively furnished by Marilyn Forbes. The downstairs area displays a bar, stage and all the furnishings necessary for an entertaining way of early western life. The upper area provides two rooms separated by a hallway and likewise furnished for an entertaining way of life. The bed quilts and hand-tooled leather holsters suspended over the bedposts were made by Marilyn.

Fig. 13–16 A small box room neatly holds all the essentials of a Barber Shop, arranged by Marilyn Forbes. Some very special items are included, such as the barber, barber's chair and shoeshine chair, which were all created by the talented Mary Kopriva.

Sources of Supply

There are numerous sources of supply that have grown by leaps and bounds. Many companies and shops are long-time advertisers and others are just beginning to bud.

This is by no means an extensive listing of sources. The few that are mentioned are meant to accommodate the newcomer to miniature crafting. Sources for other tools, lumber, trims, kits and whatever are further available through the advertisements in publications of magazines, bulletins and newsletters and through attendance at miniature shows. Always include large, self-addressed stamped envelope (SASE) when inquiring.

BEADS, FINDINGS AND NOTIONS

Boutique Trims, P.O. Drawer P, 21200 Pontiac Trail, South Lyon, MI 48178. Also egg stands, HO-scale miniatures, tools, painting and art supplies, glues and more. (Catalogue 106, $3)

Fabric-Craft Outlet, Donna Murray, 633 North Street, Middletown, NY 10940. Also buttons, fabrics, trims, laces, ribbons, miniatures and much more. (No catalogue)

JAF Miniatures, 8400 East 105th Street, Kansas City, MO 64134. Also brass bandings and miniatures. (Catalogue #3, $1.50)

BOOKS ON DOLLHOUSES, MINIATURES AND DOLLS

Paul A. Ruddell, 4701 Queensbury Road, Riverdale, MD 20840. (Catalogue free)

CONSTRUCTION MATERIALS

Architectural Model Supplies, Inc., 115-B Bellam Boulevard, P.O. Box 3497, San Rafael, CA 94902. Wood and moldings (Northeastern), trims, kits for furniture, windows, gazebo, tools, hardware, wallpaper, modular units for box rooms and more. (Catalogue, $2.50)

Carlson's Miniatures, 1 S 671 Bender Lane, West Chicago, IL 60185. Pine wood strips, components for building, including windows, doors, stairs, wood bricks, wood shakes; also pine furnishings. (Catalogue, 50¢)

Northeastern Scale Models, Inc., Box 425, Methuen, MA 01844. Northeastern products are also available through dealers. (SASE for catalogue *or* catalogue and samples, $1)

Precious Little Things, Fieldwood Company, P.O. Box 223B, Ho-Ho-Kus, NJ 07423. Components for circular staircase; building, electrical and masonry supplies; windows and greenhouses; miniature rooms and dollhouses and many crafted items. (Catalogue, $2)

Scale Model Supplies, 910 North 24th Street, Phoenix, AZ 85008. Kits for doors and windows. (Catalogue, 75¢)

Shaker Miniatures, 2913 Huntington Road, Cleveland, OH 44120. Wood and moldings (Northeastern); hardwoods; ornate moldings and trims; components for building, including windows, doors, shutters, fireplaces; hinges, tools, electric components and more. (Catalogue $1.50)

The Dollhouse Factory, Box 456, 157 Main Street, Lebanon, NJ 08833. Wood and moldings (Northeastern); hardware; hand and power tools; ready-made components and accessories; bisque dolls; books; wallpaper; kits for needlework, furniture, dollhouses and more. (Catalogue, $2)

DISPLAY BOXES OR ROOMS

Dormouse Doll Houses, One Cottage Place, Ridgewood, NJ 07450. Work is commissioned. By appointment. (No catalogue)

Joen Ellen Kanze, 26 Palmer Avenue, North White Plains, NY 10603. Custom-made rooms and dollhouses. (SASE)

The Miner's, 1825 Sterling Street North, St. Paul, MN 55109. Clock case, cherry display case, fireplace box, also eighteenth-century furniture. (Catalogue #3, $1)

The Dollhouse Factory (*see* Construction Materials)

DOLLS FOR DOLLHOUSES OR MINIATURE ROOMS

Marty Saunders, Doll Artist, 91 Surfside Road, Minot, MA 02055. Custom work, individually sculpted and dressed—*for serious collectors only.* (No catalogue, SASE)

Susan Sirkis, 11909 Blue Spruce Rd., Reston, VA 22091. Individual custom work; costumed figures—*for serious collectors only.* (No catalogue, SASE)

Winthrop Doll Workshop, Carol-Lynn Waugh, Artist, 5 Morrill Street, Winthrop, ME 04364. Porcelain originals; no reproductions; also kits. (Catalogue, 50¢ plus SASE)

ELECTRICAL APPLIANCES

Cir-Kit Concepts, Inc., 612 North Broadway, Rochester, MN 55901. A "Tape-On" wiring system. (Illustrated Catalogue, $2)

Illinois Hobbycraft, 12 South Fifth Street, Geneva, IL 60134. (75-page illustrated catalogue and list of miniature lighting dealers, $2.50 first class; $2 third class)

Illinois Hobbycraft, Inc. Instruction book: *Miniature Wiring for Doll Houses and Miniature Rooms* by Ed Leonard, 12 South Fifth Street, Geneva, IL 60134 (Paperback, $1.50)

GUIDE BOOK OF SOURCES

Guide to American Miniaturists, expanded Third Edition, Jane Haskell, 31 Evergreen Road, Northford, CN 06472. Lists 260 sources for miniatures by craftsmen and businesses. Other information included. (Softbound book is $4.25 plus 75¢ postage; hardbound book is $8 plus $1.50 postage)

NEEDLEWORK KITS

Create Your Own, Catherine Callas Knowles, Box 393, Peapack, NJ 07977. Needlepoint (petitpoint) kits for rugs, chairs, stools, bell pulls; crewel, embroidery and cross-stitch kits. (Free illustrated Catalogue, send SASE).

Doreen Sinnett Designs, 418 Santa Ana Avenue, Newport Beach, CA 92663. Mini-hooker dollhouse rug kits; also papier mâché bricks and shingles. (Free brochure, send SASE)

June Dole, 1280 North Stone Street, West Suffield, CN 06093. Cross-Stitch Kits for samplers and pillows. (Illustrated brochure, 20¢ and SASE)

Needleworks in Miniature, P.O. Box 28041, Atlanta, GA 30328. Petit-point rugs and carpets. (Illustrated brochure #3 and crewel wool color chart, $2)

SEASHELLS

Florida Supply House, P.O. Box 847, Bradenton, FL 33505. (Catalogue available)

Black Pearl, 2365 Periwinkle Way, Sanibel Island, FL 33957. Miniature seashells, natural and colored; glues. (No catalogue, send SASE)

TOOLS

Brookstone Company, 120 Vose Farm Road, Peterborough, NH 03458. In-teresting, different and fine-quality tools. (Catalogue, $1, subsequent catalogues will follow)

Dremel Manufacturing Division, 4915 21st Street, Racine, WI 53406. Power tools (use local dealer).

The Foredom Electric Company, Bethel, CN 06801. Power tools for sculpting fine detail work. (Contact local craft supplier or write for name of closest dealer)

X-acto, 4535 Van Dam Street, Long Island City, NY 11101. Basic tools, both manual and power. (Use local dealer). X-acto also furnishes shadowbox room kits, rug kits, wallpapers, moldings and more.

Some tool suppliers are listed under *Construction Materials*

WALLPAPER

J. Hermes, P.O. Box 4023, El Monte, CA 91734. (Catalogue and three $8^{1}/_{2}''$ x $11''$ designs, $2—no checks)

WOOD (COMMERCIAL)

Albert Constantine and Sons, 2050 Eastchester Road, Bronx, NY 10461. (Catalogue, 50¢)

Craftsman's Wood Service, 2727 South Mary Street, Chicago, IL 60608. (Catalogue, 50¢)

Newsletters and Publications

The Doll House and Miniature News,
3 Orchard Lane, Kirkwood, MO
63122. Publishes monthly except
summer, 10 issues; 8¹/₂" x 11"; $8.50
for third class; $9.50 for first-class
mailings.

International Dolls' House News, 56
Lincoln Wood, Haywards Heath,
Sussex, RH16 ILH. Publishes quar-
terly; 8" x 10"; overseas $8 (bills) or
$8.75 (check).

Miniature Gazette (publication of National Association of Miniature En-
thusiasts), P.O. Box 2621, Brook-
hurst Center, Anaheim, CA 92804.
Publishes quarterly; 8¹/₂" x 11"; send
SASE for membership information
which includes *Gazette.*

The Miniature Magazine, Carstens
Publications, Inc., P.O. Box 700,
Newton, NJ 07860. $1.25.

Miniature Makers Journal, 409 South
First Street, Evansville, WI 53536.
Publishes quarterly; 5¹/₂" x 8¹/₂"; $12
yearly.

Miniature Reflections, 409 South First
Street, Evansville, WI 53536. Publishes quarterly; 6³/₄" x 10"; $12
yearly.

Mott's Miniature Workshop News, P.O.
Box 5514, Sunny Hills Station, Ful-
lerton, CA 92635. Publishes an-
nually (send SASE for information).

Nutshell News, 1035 Newkirk Drive,
LaJolla, CA 92037. Publishes quarterly; 5¹/₂" x 8¹/₂"; $7 annually, over-
seas airmail $10, Canada $8, single
issue $2.

*The Scale Cabinetmaker: A Journal for
the Miniaturist,* Dorsett Miniatures,
P.O. Box 87, Pembroke, VA 24136.
Good for scale modelers. Publishes
quarterly; 8¹/₂" x 11"; $12 yearly; sin-
gle copy $3.75.

Small Talk, P.O. Box 334, Laguna
Beach, CA 92651. Publishes
monthly; 8¹/₂" x 11"; 12 issues for
$10 yearly, international rate is $15.

Bibliography

GENERAL BOOKS

Aronson, Joseph. *The Encyclopedia of Furniture*. Crown Publishers, 1965.

Burchard, John, and Bush-Brown, Albert. *The Architecture of America: A Social and Cultural History*. Little, Brown and Co. 1961.

Congdon, Herbert Wheaton. *Early American Homes for Today*. Charles E. Tuttle Company, 1963.

Daniele, Joseph. *Building Early American Furniture*. Stackpole Books, 1974.

Darty, Peter. *Chairs: A Guide to Choosing, Buying and Collecting*. Pyne Press, 1972.

Davidson, Marshall B. *The American Heritage History of Notable American Houses*. American Heritage Publishing Co., 1971.

Fitch, James Marston. *Architecture and the Esthetics of Plenty*. Columbia University Press, 1961.

Gottshall, Franklin H. *Reproducing Antique Furniture*. Crown Publishers, 1971.

Ormsbee, Thomas H. *Field Guide to American Victorian Furniture*. Bonanza Books, *n.d.*

——— *Field Guide to Early American Furniture*. Little, Brown and Co., 1951.

Sitwell, Sacheverell (editor). *Great Houses of Europe*. G. P. Putnam's Sons, 1961.

Wallace, Philip B. *Colonial Houses: Pre-Revolutionary Period*. Bonanza Books, 1931.

Waterman, Thomas Tileston. *The Dwellings of Colonial America*. The University of North Carolina Press, *n.d.*

Williams, Henry Lionel and Ottalie K. *America's Small Houses*. Bonanza Books, *n.d.*

——— *Great Houses of America*. G. P. Putnam's Sons, 1969.

Zook, Nicholas. *Houses of New England Open to the Public*. Barre Publishing Co., 1968.

82 *Distinctive Houses from Architectural Record*. F.W. Dodge Corp., 1952.

DOLLHOUSE BOOKS

Farlie, Barbara L., and Clarke, Charlotte L. *All About Doll Houses*. Bobbs-Merrill Co., 1975.

Jacobs, Flora Gill. *A History of Dolls' Houses*. Charles Scribner's Sons, 1965.

———*Dolls' Houses in America*. Charles Scribner's Sons, 1974.

—— *A World of Doll Houses*. Rand McNally & Co., 1965.

Jackson, Valerie, and Flick, Pauline. *The Dollhouse Idea Book*. Hawthorne Books, 1974.

Johnson, Audrey. *Furnishing Dolls' Houses*. Charles T. Branford Co., 1972.

MacLaren, Catherine B. *This Side of Yesterday in Miniature*. Nutshell News, 1975.

McElroy, Joan. *Doll's House Furniture Book*. Alfred A. Knopf, 1976.

Newman, Thelma R., and Merrill, Virginia. *The Complete Book of Miniatures*. Crown Publishers, 1975.

O'Brien, Marion Maeve. *The Collector's Guide to Dollhouses and Dollhouse Miniatures*. Hawthorne Books, 1974.

—— *Make Your Own Dollhouses and Dollhouse Miniatures*. Hawthorne Books, 1975.

—— *Make and Furnish Your Own Miniature Rooms*. Hawthorne Books, 1976.

Ruthberg, Helen Karp. *The Book of Miniatures: Furniture and Accessories*. Chilton Book Co., 1977.

Thorne, Mrs. James Ward. *American Rooms in Miniature* (1941) and *European Rooms in Miniature* (1962). The Art Institute of Chicago.

—— *Miniature Rooms at The Phoenix Art Museum*, 1972.

Worrell, Estelle Ansley. *The Dollhouse Book*. D. Van Nostrand Co., 1966.

Dollhouse Miniatures. Carstens Publications, 1975.

The Miniature Magazine. Carstens Publications, 1976, 1977.

Index

Page numbers in **bold type** refer to information found in illustrations

169

Jack Ruthberg, photograph

HELEN KARP RUTHBERG

Helen was born in Syracuse, New York. With an avid interest in art, she majored in illustration and graduated from Syracuse University.

Learning the fundamentals of advertising art through employment in various media, she made her niche in department store advertising, from fashions to furniture, and in pharmaceutical advertising, from layouts to finished art. She also enjoyed free-lance designing of greeting cards and shopping bags.

Although she works in all fine art media, she enjoys the challenge of watercolor, pre-ferring this medium above all others. Her paintings are in several private collections and have been exhibited in many regional shows. Her one-woman show at the Arts Council of Orange County, New York State, was a combination exhibition of watercolors and miniature rooms. The show attracted over 3,000 viewers and Helen admits that the miniatures were the principal reason.

She has also exhibited paintings with The Miniature Painters, Sculptors and Gravers Society of Washington, D.C., receiving awards.

Crafting is another of Helen's talents; she works in shellcraft, dried pressed flowers, three-dimensional paper tole, felt work and more. Several of her articles, dealing with some of these subjects, have been published by *Creative Crafts* magazine and *The Miniature Magazine*.

She authored *The Book of Miniatures: Furniture and Accessories*, which was selected by three different book clubs.

Other pastimes are crewel embroidery and sewing and she often makes her own clothes. But her most enjoyable diversion is flying with her physician husband, who pilots their own plane.

She resides in Middletown, New York, for northern climate and in Boynton Beach, Florida, for southern exposure, which also just happens to be closer to her son, a medical student.